a YEAR in

KRONOBERG

(It's in SWEDEN)

geoff BUNN

January

The year began with snow. Lots of snow. And our 200-metre long drive, which had seemed such an attractive feature only a few months before, now felt like a 200-metre long wall cutting us off from the rest of the world. The more we looked at it, the longer it seemed to get.

Beyond that wall, at the end of the drive, we could see that the road was more or less clear.

But Sweden was like that. Functional and efficient even in the face of a hostile climate. Snowploughs passed two or three times a day to keep things moving, and although roads remained off-white rather than tarmac-grey, they were almost all kept open.

Sadly for us though, such invitingly clear roads might as well have been on the moon. The closest supermarket was about 25 minutes away and the drive, our snow covered escape, was the only way out for our car. Although the nearest shop, in the village centre 15 minutes' walk away, did sell many basics, the only superstore within walking distance was a garden machinery centre. And even if we had suddenly discovered an irresistible urge to buy some oil for the lawnmower or invest in a new pair of secateurs, that, too, would have been a long, cold hike.

We needed the car. So there was only one thing for it; the snow would have to be cleared.

Fortunately, when my wife and I had bought the property, the previous owners had had the courtesy – common to all Swedes – to leave behind one or two essential items. These included a fridge freezer, a cooker, a sit-on lawnmower and, more pertinently, a snow blower. So it was down to the garage, to dig out the snow blower, that I now went.

Snow blowers, for those who have never seen one, look rather like a cross between a pram and a small tractor. They have a big scoop on the front, which collects the snow, and a sort of chimney affair which then blows the snow out to either side as the machine is pushed forwards. The wheels are huge. Very much like those of a miniature tractor.

"This will clear the drive in no time", I insisted, as my wife, Emma, watched me with some apprehension from the front porch. Her apprehension was well founded. I was a more than competent DIYer with an engineering background, but snow - like patience - was something I had very little experience of.

"Isn't it a bit small for such a long drive?" she finally asked, "The snow is pretty deep. Won't it be too much for the thing?"

I ignored this doom-laden prediction and prepared to start 'the thing' up.

The snow blower was one of those machines that have to be started by pulling a cord. I have never found such things to start easily and, true to form, it didn't start easily today either. In fact after about five minutes or so of pulling the cord, and removing layer after layer of clothes as I got increasingly hot, it still hadn't spluttered into life. In fact, it had barely spluttered at all.

"Perhaps it's too cold for it?" Emma suggested.

"Don't be daft", I said. "What would be the point of a snow blower that only worked in warm weather? It'll be fine".

After another five minutes of tugging on the cord and swearing, sure enough, it did finally start. And with some effort, and not a little pride, off I went, along the drive, scooping and blowing snow to the left and right of me.

For a short time, too short a time, I felt like the Vikings must have felt when they first splashed ashore in England a thousand years ago. I was the boss here. This was triumph. And as the snow parted to make way for me, I felt that I was somehow getting my own back for us British.

Alas, 20 minutes later – with less than a quarter of the job done – the snow blower was looking and acting decidedly tired. And so was I. Snow blowing was hard work. Too hard for me, unused to the cold as I was, and, so it seemed, too hard for the snow blower too.

"I'm never going to clear this lot", I said to Emma, as she brought me out a cup of tea, which cooled faster than I could drink it, "I'll be here all day. I'm already exhausted".

Emma had a go too, probably clearing more than I had and in a faster time. And then I did a little bit more as well. But despite our combined efforts, still almost half of the drive remained stubbornly covered in a thick blanket of snow.

Reluctant to fail in Sweden upon our first heavy snowfall, however, we were not going to be beaten by this, and we determined that by taking it in turns we would get the drive cleared. And so we pressed on.

Sadly the snow blower didn't have the same steely resolution. It had been here before. Knew the score. And clearly didn't fancy another winter moving snow around. And with 40 or so metres still to clear, it wheezed to a full stop.

We kicked it a bit. As one does when they have no idea what they are doing. Tutted at it. Tweaked a button. Examined a cable. Kicked it again. Looked around for inspiration. Found none. And gave up.

"Let's go and have a sandwich and then come back and finish it off with the shovels", Emma suggested. "Surely, between the two of us, we can do that last bit?"

So in we went.

And just as we closed the door, the sky darkened. And down came yet more snow.

We sat at the window thoughtfully, eating our sandwiches and watching it fall. It wasn't like English snow. It wasn't just little bits of the stuff. Not damp, not reluctant to fall. Not small flakes or grains, but great, vast fluffy feather-like clouds of snow, coming down so thick and fast that we had barely two metres of visibility.

"It'll stop in a minute", I said, after a little while.

We finished our sandwiches. We drank our tea. We had a piece of cake and another cup of tea, periodically getting up to peer through the window. And all the while, the snow still fell.

The last sight we had of the drive, four hours later as the daylight turned into darkness, was of the distant faint shape of the snow blower, abandoned by the side of the drive and disappearing under the thick white duvet and resembling, for all the world, a snow covered tombstone; a memorial to our first attempt at snow clearing.

*

Sweden isn't everyone's first choice as a holiday destination. And it's probably even further down the list of targets for a permanent move, never getting a mention on one of those 'Follow the Sun' type programmes that invite everyone to upsticks and move abroad.

This may all be down to short summers and long cold winters. But other factors, such as the robust supply of mosquitoes and the vast empty tracts of impenetrable forest, must surely play a role as well.

Then again, it isn't all snow and *skog* (the Swedish word for forest).

For a start Swedes are infinitely polite, well educated and they love outdoor activities. If you want to ski, sail, swim or walk in peace and quiet, then this is the country for you. As a matter of fact, by law, you are allowed – and even encouraged – to swim in any lake, canoe on any water and walk just about anywhere you want as long as you don't trample on crops or someone's meticulously tidy flowerbeds.

The country is huge too. And massively under-populated. In an area four or five times the size of England, the population is less than that of Greater London. Just ten million people in all that space.

Admittedly, a good deal of that emptiness is the aforementioned *skog*. Which is almost wholly the domain of the lumberjack, the moose and the bear. (And, yes, also of the aforementioned mosquito.) And a good deal of what remains is actually water, Sweden having over 90,000 lakes.

But the towns – when you can find one – are safe and clean. Streets are often almost empty of cars and busy with pushbikes. Food is no more expensive than in the UK. Beer can be bought readily in bars or supermarkets, despite what one may have heard to the contrary. And the people are warm, welcoming and almost all, to a man, woman and child, fluent in English; a factor that we were to find useful time and time again.

In the end though, it was none of those things that took us to Sweden. We moved to the county of Kronoberg, in Sweden because, surprisingly, the country seemed to have the most affordable housing in Western Europe. And we were not rich.

The EU had opened up the continent, allowing us all to move anywhere. And we decided to take advantage of that and sell up our flat in the UK and buy a house outright instead. A house in the country. We couldn't afford to do that in the UK. And, as we looked around property in France and Spain and so on, it didn't really look like we could afford to do it there either. Then I hit on the idea of Sweden. And we soon found that if we sold up in the UK, we could go to Sweden and buy a pretty large detached house, with a lot of land, and still have enough money left to live on for a year or so whilst we found work.

And why not? We both loved the idea of getting out of the fast lane, which life in the UK certainly was, and finding somewhere where life was a little slower. And then there was all that land. Surely, we'd find some use for it. We were both keen gardeners – or at least I enjoyed gardening and Emma enjoyed sitting outdoors...

*

The following morning, the snow had finally stopped falling.

Along the drive, there was no longer any sign whatsoever of the snow blower. It hadn't been stolen. It had simply been completely buried under the fresh fall of snow. And, as things would turn out, it was going to stay there until the spring.

So much for that.

I trudged down to the cellar, took out a shovel, and walked out onto the drive. All I had to do was clear 200 metres, with a shovel, every time it snowed. True, that meant that life was going to get very 'samey'. But it was either that or starve.

And so I began.

Immediately the sound of shovel scraping on snow took me back to my childhood. I recalled, now somewhat wistfully, how people used to make that sound when they cleared the pavement outside their homes in the city. But that was once or twice each winter.

Scrape, scrape, scrape. Pavements of a mere 5 or 10 metres in length. Usually with no more than a few centimetres of snow. And even that was often considered a chore; something that caused the occasional argument or would be used, by more crafty parents, as the snow for the children's snowman. I paused and looked up. I still had the best part of 200 metres to clear and we had no children to persuade to clear it all for me. In any case, how big would the snowman be? I did a quick calculation in my head... and it worked out that I had about 5,000 m3 of snow to clear. Any snowman made from that lot would be visible from outer space!

Suddenly the thought occurred to me that if I could just clear most of the drive, I might be able to find the snow blower, drag it back to the garage, repair it, fire it up again and finish the job off with that. Doing all of that, preferably, before the next heavy fall of snow.

With that idea in mind I began scraping and digging with a newfound vigour. And in just twenty minutes I had cleared all of about 10 metres. Then, suddenly, I heard the sound of another snow blower. It was our neighbour, Edvard. Our only neighbour, admittedly, and he lived a good 500 metres away. But a neighbour all the same.

Looking down at how little progress I was making, I decided it was time to go and ask for some of that famous Scandinavian hospitality and helpfulness. (At this point, I should add, that though friendly and helpful, Swedes do not socialise willingly with people they do not already know. So it was not at all unusual that we had yet to speak to our neighbour even though we had already been in our new home for over a month.)

Edvard was an elderly man who appeared to live alone and he was indeed busy clearing his own drive with a smart new snow blower. He had one or two distinct advantages over me – his drive was no more than a few metres long and, having been born and brought up in this part of Sweden, he was more than used to dealing with snow.

As he saw me approach he switched the machine off and gave me a small wave.

We said hello (in Sweden hello is '*Hej*' which is pronounced as 'Hey'), introduced ourselves by first name, which is something all Swedes do, and then we exchanged a few polite words about the weather. Which seemed to be something else all Swedes do. He nodded knowingly when I told him that we were indeed stranded behind our 'wall' of snow.

He smiled a little when I told him of our experiences so far at trying to clear it – all of which I was able to do in English, which made things so much easier – and a broader smile passed across his face before he nodded seriously again and said, "Have you not seen Johan over it? You can phone him. I have his number. I know that he has a new tractor now for working in the skog and he can manage almost anything with this I think".

Without another word, just a quick nod of his head in the general direction of his front door, Edvard then led me indoors.

This was a first for me. I had never been inside a Swedish home before (other than my own). Fortunately I did vaguely recall from somewhere or other that one must always remove one's shoes or boots when entering a home, and this I did just in time to be offered a large pair of extremely thick, woollen, guest-socks.

The need for this de-booting isn't as strange as it may at first appear; most Swedish homes have solid parquet flooring and dirt, twigs, bits of gravel or what have you – not to mention great clumps of snow – would be likely to damage it.

Edvard's somewhat overly warm home was festooned with paintings and photographs. And many of the latter must have been his family, because they bore a striking resemblance to this chisel-featured Nordic man. There also seemed to be an enormous quantity of chairs and places to sit and I found myself briefly wondering if Edvard had a deep-rooted need to sit in different places at different times of the day for some reason. Or was it that he frequently held dinner parties or card schools? In fact, as the year went by, I found that this was a feature common to most Swedish homes; chairs were 'in'.

"Here, I knew I had the number", Edvard said, suddenly interrupting my thoughts, and coming back into the room with a sheaf of papers. "Johan is a good man and he will do you a good job". He paused. "First you must take a little something to drink? To help you with the cold."

That sounded good to me. And I agreed, taking one of the many seats and expecting a spot of Aquavit or something similar. I had had Aquavit once before and recalled its fiery taste fondly. Or then again perhaps it would be vodka? Absolut Vodka is made in Sweden, and not very far from where we were now living. Either would have been fine by me.

20 minutes later, having had only a very weak and rather milky coffee and a few unbelievably sugary biscuits, I was ready to leave Edvard's and get back to my snow.

At the door I thanked Edvard for the information. We exchanged a few more words about the weather – which he was very keen to analyse and compare with previous Januarys in much the same way that English people endlessly discuss the climate – and then I trudged back across the snowy wasteland clutching Johan's telephone number firmly in my hand.

Once home I telephoned Johan.

Two hours later the ground began to shake.

"What on earth is that?" I asked, finding myself wondering suddenly if they had earthquakes in Sweden, and whether that was perhaps why so few people lived here.

"Erm... there seems to be a yellow house coming down the drive", said Emma.

Indeed there was something. And although it wasn't a house, it was certainly the same size as a house. Johan had arrived with his new tractor; the cause of the shaking ground. An enormous great machine, in bright yellow, with flashing orange lights on top.

He came along the drive at more or less full speed, for all the world as if there was no snow at all lying on it, let alone the now almost two metres of the stuff there actually was. His machine stopped a short distance from the house and we went out to say hello.

Johan had a very large machine. That was true. But the man himself was also huge. Fully seven feet tall, and almost as broad, he made us immediately feel sorry for our British ancestors who had had to face such giants coming ashore in their long ships all those centuries ago. No wonder the Ancient British used to run away at the first sight of those square sails.

"Hallo! Johan!" he said, extending an immense hand towards us. "You have some snow to be cleared?"

"Umm... yes", said Emma, offering her hand and introducing herself and then, looking past Johan at the drive behind him, "Well, there was some. But you seem to have cleared it already".

Johan smiled, nodded at the cleared snow, and said, "Was that all there was to be done? Ah, that was not a problem. I will clear it more when I drive away." And that was that. A few notes changed hands. Yet more comments about the weather (which I was now aware the Swedes were truly fascinated by) and off he went. Taking the yellow monster with him.

Two days, one snow blower – now buried even deeper in the snow which Johan had swept aside – and countless hours of work by us. All that had failed to clear the drive. Giant Johan did it, with his giant machine, in the time it took him to drive 200 metres.

From then on, we promised ourselves, Johan would always have the job.

*

The middle of January saw no change in the weather. It was extremely cold and it snowed heavily on most days. But as this no longer prevented us from getting out and about, we quickly grew accustomed to it and even began to enjoy it.

For a start, the thick snow, covering trees and houses, was beautiful. Quite wonderful. Branches hung down like great frozen plumes of white fur, wilting and occasionally letting fall heavy clumps of snow with a dull thud. Fields – where there were fields, which were few and far between as most of Sweden is forest – seemed to merge seamlessly with the sky. On one day, both a flat sheet of grey. On another both a dazzling white. Only on days where the sky was blue could the two be distinguished.

And then there were animal tracks of all kinds. These were an endless source of fascination for us. We had no idea, as yet, what most of them were, but we worried from time to time that some of them might be something dangerous. Coming from the UK, where the most dangerous animal was probably the hedgehog, we were surprised to learn that there were over 3,000 wild bears in Sweden. And a good number of wolves too. We soon discovered that wolves and bear didn't live in Kronoberg, which was a relief, but there were countless numbers of wild boar around here and even the odd lynx. Neither of whom we were overly keen to meet in the garden.

Then there was the silence. It was almost hypnotic. Certainly it was soporific. Kronoberg is not the most noisy of places at any time. Although situated pretty far south in the country, where most of Sweden's population, industry and agriculture is also found, Kronoberg is a much emptier region than its neighbours. Largely forest, with some lakes big enough to be seen from space, outside the towns and away from the few busy roads, it's unusual to hear any noise other than distant chain saws, or perhaps a tractor working one of the few small clearings in the woods. But the snow brought even those sounds to a standstill. And apart from the noise of the post van delivering mail, or perhaps the odd deer (at least, we hoped it was a deer) barking in the distance, nothing stirred.

For us, coming from the UK, where snow causes chaos and silence is no longer heard, this new calm-bringing and silent yet usable world of snow was a delight.

But there were still many icy surprises in store. And one Sunday afternoon, taking a soon to become regular trip to a local factory outlet store – which was hugely popular and yet also wondrously quiet – we stopped the car for a little while by a frozen lake.

We had imagined that driving on snow would be difficult. We had both experienced the near-impossibility of steering in Britain when the annual inch or two of snow fell and traffic came to a halt. But in Sweden, driving in snow just isn't a problem. In part, this is because they expect the stuff. So they have countless thousands of snowploughs and tractors with plough attachments for keeping the roads clear. But, much more than that, it is also because there is a legal obligation for all cars to wear snow tyres from the beginning of December until the end of March. So driving – specifically steering – wasn't a problem. With studs on the tyres, the car just responded as if it was still on clean, dry tarmac.

But there were other means of transport too. And we were watching one of them now.

The lake was big by any measure, and surrounded by almost unbroken forest. It couldn't have had a more naturally attractive setting.

But today, frozen as it was, the lake was the scene of an ice hockey match. An informal match, from what we could gather, as the teams seemed to consist of men, woman and children of all shapes and sizes. And there appeared to be a good deal more players in one team than there were in the other.

We stood on the shore of the lake and watched for a while as people raced back and forth on skates, chasing a small disc-like object with sticks. And we wondered whether the ice was really strong enough to support such vigorous activity. On the one hand clearly, it was, as these good folk seemed wholly confident in its ability to hold them all and let them all dash about wildly. On the other hand, from time to time there were eerie noises from the ice. It creaked or cracked a little and sometimes a lot. It made strange echoing noises like great plates of metal being scraped against each other. And, in truth, we were both very glad that we couldn't skate and so weren't tempted to go out there on the ice. Not least because we had no idea how deep the water was. Underneath. Down there in the cold, dark, icy depths.

Apart from the freestyle hockey players there were other people out on the ice too, here and there in little groups of two or three. For all the world looking like folk sitting around a bonfire – only without a bonfire. We watched them for a while too, wondering what they were doing. It looked like an awfully cold pastime to sit around non-existent fires on frozen sheets of water. But then when one of them walked past us carrying something small and silver we realised that they were actually fishing – and catching fish! – through holes in the ice.

Still none of this tempted us to stray from the shore and out onto that creaking white wilderness. But when two tiny children tottered out onto the ice with what could easily have been their great-grandfather, we did start to feel that we were letting the side down. Surely, we agreed, if it is safe enough for toddlers and such grand old pensioners, then we ought to do our bit for Britain and go out onto the ice too?

And so out we went.

And over I went. Without any hesitation whatsoever.

The trouble was that ice is ice, even in countries where most people are capable of walking, running, fishing or even playing hockey on it. And this ice was no exception. It was slippery. Very slippery. And although I consoled myself a little by saying out loud "I'd like to see how they deal with our endless rain!", I did feel more than a bit useless.

Emma, by contrast, did not fall over. She walked, gingerly, though admittedly upright, all of five or six steps from the bank. She turned. Almost gracefully. And smiled.

And then the ice creaked.

And she fled in terror back to the bank.

Well that was enough of that. We felt we had at least given it a
try. As for the rest, well, we didn't know the rules of ice hockey
anyway. So there would have been little to gain in walking further
out and getting stuck into the match. We'd probably only have
hurt someone, we assured each other. Possibly not even ourselves.
And as to the fishing? I enjoyed fishing. I had spent many hours
doing that back in England. Hot sunny days watching a bright
orange float. But that was a world away from staring at a small
black hole in the ice.

And so it was with our ignorance that we justified our fear of the
ice and stayed put on solid ground. Anyway, the shop would close
in another hour or so. We had things to buy. So we bravely left
them all to it.

*

We soon found that one of the great things about living in Sweden
was the central heating, which really was second to none.

For a start, there were all kinds of options available. Homes could
be heated with electric heaters or wood-burning stoves. The first
of these was expensive, though, and the second could be quite a
chore.

But there were other weird and wonderful ideas too: for instance,
there was something called a *Fjärrvärme* (pronounced a little like
'Fair Warmer' though with a letter v instead of a w). This was a
kind of communal central heating system which was provided by

the local council as a by-product from local industry. Inevitably even the environmentally aware Swedes produced some waste from their factories, and one of the ways they dealt with this was by recycling waste heat and using it to warm up local houses. It was cheap. Clean. And it was growing in popularity. Unfortunately, it was also only available in certain areas.

Then there was something called a *Bergvärme* – which took heat from underground and brought it into your home. The installation of one of these things seemed to require drilling a 20-foot deep hole in your floor or something like that, and then circulating water down into the hole and back. It all sounded pretty risky and rather far-fetched but, in truth, the hole was very narrow and, once the boiler or whatever it was was placed on top of the hole, you had no idea it was there. And although the whole thing made very little sense to us, by all accounts, one of these things could save you quite a bit of money on your heating and would add value to your property which more than covered the installation costs. Sadly they wouldn't really heat a large house – which ours was.

For larger homes there were two viable options: oil central heating and central heating provided by wood pellets. The first of these was rapidly going out of fashion as oil prices seemed intent on rising ever higher. It was also known as the dirty choice and was now severely frowned upon by most Swedes. The second, however, was becoming quite the thing. Sweden has nothing if not millions of trees. And those trees are regularly cut down and turned into things like flat-packed furniture, cardboard to package the same and paper to tell you how to put it all together. Fashionable and practical as all that was, it had meant for a long time that there was a whole lot of waste in the form of pretty useless sawdust. But then a bright spark had realised that if that sawdust was compressed into little pellets and given a whirl in a large tumble-drier, it – or rather they, the pellets – could be burnt to heat homes and provide hot water for a pretty minimal cost.

We had never had central heating provided in such a renewable fashion before, and the idea of these endlessly recyclable wood-sawdust-pellets appealed to us. So one of the first things we had to do to the house, in terms of modernisation, was to go out and buy a small device that attached to the front of the central heating boiler and allowed us to burn these pellets.

It should be noted at this point that Swedish central heating boilers are nothing at all like British central heating boilers. In the UK, a boiler usually lives in a cupboard on the landing. And it is quite happy there. But in Sweden this would be impractical for a number of reasons. For a start, the Swedish boiler – like so much in Sweden – is super-sized. About the size of a small car. And installing that in a cupboard on the landing would lead to only one thing: a collapsed first floor. But there was more to it than that, as we were soon to find out.

Because wood pellets don't come in small envelopes or little paper sacks. They don't arrive by post. They aren't lightweight. In fact they come by the pallet full. 16 kg per sack. And 48 sacks to the pallet. (That's 768 kg in total or more than 3/4 of a ton for those of you who still think in those terms!) And all of those sacks contain thousands of dusty pellets. So the very last place you would want to store them is anywhere near your bedroom or airing cupboard.

Consequently, in addition to the small device that has to be fitted to the front of the central heating boiler, a large silver coloured container – to hold all the pellets – has to stand next to the boiler and trickle-feed the thing. That means the whole lot, weighing close to a thousand kilograms, has to live in the cellar.

Once again, however, the Swedes seem to have thought of this well in advance. And their cellars, unlike British cellars, are huge, often containing a table tennis room, toilet, shower, sometimes a guest bedroom or even a sauna. And so, thereby, plenty of space for a full-scale semi-industrial central heating boiler and lots of extra trappings.

It didn't take long to buy the parts to set up our central heating. They were delivered within a few days and we installed them ourselves and, apart from dropping a large metal part on my own foot, it all went without a hitch.

We were now ready to take delivery of our first lot of pellets.

Locally the pellets were distributed by a farmer who, in winter, along with most Swedish farmers we imagined, was not overly burdened. Fields were under snow and livestock, never on a huge scale in Sweden, spent the whole winter in barns the size of aircraft hangers, and apart from taking them food and collecting the cow's milk, there didn't seem to be a lot else anyone could do. Diversification was clearly the name of the game and this particular farmer had diversified into being 'the pellet man'.

"His name is Ulf", said Emma as she put the phone down, having ordered our pellets.

"Ulf?", I repeated a little incredulously. "Are there really people called Ulf?" It sounded a very Vikingy sort of name to us.

The following morning Ulf and his machinery appeared on our drive.

And although Ulf's tractor was decidedly miniature compared to that of Johan 'the snow clearer', Ulf himself, just like Johan, was another Scandinavian giant.

"Hallo! Hallo!" he beamed, as he climbed down from his cab, "And welcome to Sweden! Ulf. This is your first winter here?"

"Yes", we replied, as we shook hands with yet another giant and introduced ourselves. "Yes, it is our first winter".

"Well you have done the best thing to order pellets, they will keep you warm for sure. They are the best thing. And our winters can be maybe cold sometimes."

"Maybe cold?" said Emma. Last night on the radio we had heard that it was currently -12 °C where we were living.

"Ah yes", said Ulf. "Not like now. This is not so bad". He was in what seemed to be the thinnest of jackets. "But they say it will turn cold next week. Twenty eight minus degrees."

And with that he gave us a big smile.

Normally there would probably have been a few more exchanges about the snow, the temperature and the forecast for the week ahead but we were visibly turning blue in the cold and, after all, there was pellet business to attend to.

Ulf's tractor pulled a substantial trailer which was stacked high with our two pallets of pellets. They appeared much larger in terms of size and quantity than we had expected and we looked at them with some trepidation. Fortunately Ulf was not the kind of man to leave people to struggle. And as he manoeuvred the things off the trailer, with a forklift attachment mounted on the front of the tractor, he paused and shouted down to us, "Where would you like that I put them? Not here in the snow, for sure?"

We pointed at the garage doors that led to the cellar under the house. These doors were very much smaller than Ulf, never mind his tractor or the 48 sacks of pellets.

"Can you put them in there?" I asked hopefully.

Ulf looked. "Yes, I will be able to do that. No problem."

And so – much to our relief – he did. With a deft touch he was easily able to manipulate the pallets so that they ended up sitting just inside our garage door, in the dry and warm.

That little extra touch, which he was in no way obliged to do, cheered us up no end. We paid him, in cash, for the pellets and off he went, partially clearing the snow from the drive as he went.

"Well that wasn't too bad", I said to Emma. "Shall we go and have a cup of tea?"

"Erm... there's just one thing", said Emma. She turned and pointed at our car which was sitting out on the drive, slowly disappearing beneath the freshly falling snow. "How do we put the car away in the garage now that all those sacks of pellets are sitting right inside the door?"

Unfortunately she was quite right. We couldn't leave the car outside all night with temperatures forecast to drop down ever further. But until we shifted all those pellets from the garage into the boiler room, the car was going nowhere.

And so the month ended much as it had begun, with a good deal of hard physical graft. Only this time, instead of it being necessary in order for us to be able to get the car out and go and buy a loaf of bread, it was necessary in order to for us to put the car to bed.

There was one advantage. This time, instead of our having to work outside, clearing snow, we had to work inside, moving sack after sack after sack after sack of little wooden pellets.

Needless to say we slept extraordinarily well that night.

February

The nearest village, our village, was fifteen minutes' walk away along a quiet road. A proper country lane, in fact. Traffic in the lane was light all year round but it was even lighter when the snow was falling.

All the same, we preferred to walk along the snow covered bridle path that connected our house to the village, partly because it was prettier, like something off a Christmas card, and partly because immense double trucks carrying hundreds of tree trunks occasionally used the otherwise virtually empty road.

These trucks, and their great cargoes of wood, were the produce of and for the Swedish timber industry. They owned the country. More or less. This was their world. Not ours. And they were scary enough when seen from a distance, never mind close up. So we used the bridle path.

The village itself consisted of two long rows of detached houses, either side of the road, in a mix of styles. Some houses were built of brick – or at least faced with brick. Some were built of concrete blocks and then faced with a very rough looking plaster. Some were built of wood. And the rest were a mixture of stone and timber.

The brick and concrete properties usually dated back to around the 1950s or 1960s. Typically they were a rather nauseous yellow or an equally unpleasant off-white. Squareish, often almost industrial in appearance, with large windows and prominent garages, these houses lacked any obvious charm and neither Emma nor I liked the style. Whenever we saw one of these houses, we half imagined an interior still done out in the style of that period. As it turned out, when we did have cause to go into one of these functional houses one day, it was indeed still done out in decor from the 1970s. But that is another story...

The timber or timber and stone properties were altogether different. Older – often very much older – they captured what, for us, was the essence of Swedish architectural design. Built from the material so abundant here, namely wood, some of these houses had carved, white-painted fretwork around the windows or along the eaves. They usually had small windows further divided up by muntins. Many also had heavy and ancient looking wooden doors which, although invariably handsome, usually looked ill-fitting and we imagined that the drafts inside must be fierce.

Sometimes the whole framework of the house, being made of timber, was crooked to a greater or lesser extent due to age. One house in particular, although presumably originally built on one level, had so warped through the centuries that it now seemed to have an Escher-like quality to it. And we suspected that to go from one end of the house to the other there would now have to be steps in the middle of the house. Certainly a marble dropped on the floor inside would have rolled the full length of the property.

Unlike the more functional houses, the wooden houses also seemed to be a mix of colours. Some were a particularly lurid blue. Some yellow. One or two were even a pale pistachio green. The smartest were black or white. But, by far and away, the most common colour was a deep browny-red called Falun red, named after the town in central Sweden where the pigment was first produced from the copper which was mined there in abundance.

Although this red could look quite glorious against a blue sky, it struck us as being a dismal sort of colour in many weather conditions and we wondered why it was so popular. Against the dark green of the forest in particular, it was a gloomy red. And we could see why shades like bright yellow were also common.

The red colouration of the timber homes was not the only Swedish architectural feature that took our eye. Back in the autumn, while looking for a house to buy, we had noticed a strange open plan character to Swedish towns and villages.

Most houses were surrounded by large spreading lawns, but these lawns were usually totally un-fenced and gardens often lacked even so much as a low hedge or wire, so that the houses all appeared to share a single enormous garden. How young children knew where to stop playing with their brightly coloured plastic tractors in order to avoid crossing into their neighbours' gardens, and how the dogs knew which flowerbeds to use and which belonged to the neighbour, were questions we couldn't answer. We assumed it spoke of something deep within the Scandinavian character. It was as if they didn't want to show off, to suggest that they had a larger garden than the people next door. It was also as if they didn't want to cut themselves off either. When the winter came in, the dark and the cold, perhaps it was nice to know that other people were close by, and perhaps a heavy snow-laden hedge would negate that impression.

In the centre of our own village, just past an orphaned burial ground which seemed to have graves but no church, there was also a shop. A multi-purpose village store-cum-post-office-cum-café.

Two or three years previously, the shop had been threatened with closure. The occupants – both by then in their late 80s – had retired, and no single individual had wanted to take the place on. So a sort of action group had been formed from among the more community minded of the villagers, and they had somehow persuaded the local council to help subsidise the place in order to keep it open.

That was then. A few years on, and the council had been all but repaid. The shop was now thriving and a focal point for the village. Many other villages, by all accounts, had not been so fortunate.

Whether this particular shop would have thrived quite as well without Carina, however, was another matter.

Carina was every man's idea of the perfect Swedish woman. She was pretty, she was blonde, she was blue-eyed and she was sun-tanned even in the depths of the winter. She was also extremely hard working and probably the friendliest, most easy-going person we had ever met. And it struck us as no coincidence that the majority of customers who spent a half-hour drinking weak coffee and eating cakes in the café corner of the slightly cramped shop space were men. Indeed it was not at all unusual to see four tractors and a couple of strange forestry machines in the car park and to find all the male drivers sitting inside and chatting to Carina.

In my first few weeks in Sweden, thanks to Carina, I had suddenly become very keen to pop along to the local shop. I had been up for stamps. Then willingly gone back for a loaf or two of bread. Then I agreed to just go up for some chocolate. Then another loaf of bread or a packet of something. And then a few more stamps. Unfortunately none of this had gone unnoticed. "I wondered why you were so keen to go to the shop", Emma said, a few days after her first meeting with Carina. "It's not normally the sort of thing you volunteer to go and do!"

But Carina took it all in her stride. When the electricity went out in the shop, which it did more than once, as snow caused a tree branch to fall on the power lines, she would light a few candles and carry on working. When things were dropped or broken in the shop by accident, she didn't blink an eye. She was and she demonstrated, in all respects, the perfect example of what the Swedish call *"Lagom"* or a relaxed un-worriedness; a trait common to most Swedes. Nothing seemed to faze her. Not really. And it was only when it came to working out the postal costs to Britain from Sweden, or the price of sending a parcel to France or Germany that she got completely and utterly lost and usually had to be helped by the customer. Which meant, more often than not, that the customer had to go behind the counter and fill in the forms and weigh the parcels and reckon up the costs while Carina took five minutes off to have a cup of coffee with the men from the forestry commission.

It was during one of these pauses, as Emma went behind the counter and dealt with the postage for herself, that Carina took a break and told me, over a cup of the weak coffee which seemed to be everywhere in Sweden, about Farfarn: Farfarn was a man with a very long white beard who sounded like he resembled Father Christmas.

According to Carina, Farfarn would occasionally give visitors to the area quite a fright by suddenly emerging from the forest, looking a little bedraggled and often carrying a large gun.

I told her I could see why a gun-toting Father Christmas might scare people. But Carina assured me that Farfarn was kindness and gentleness personified and that he carried the gun "just for hunting the birds or a deer perhaps". And in near perfect English she continued, "Farfarn lives out in the skog. In his cabin. He has no car and no electricity. And he only comes in to shop here once every two months. He comes with his horse and a thing it pulls..."

"A cart?"

"Yes. A cart. And then he buys just provisions for himself and some times one or two things for the horse. Then he will go again for some more weeks."

"How does he live?" I asked, wondering how anyone could get by in this day and age by making only a single bi-monthly appearance in a shop and not having such things as the internet. "Does he work?"

"He farms some small pieces of land. He fishes a little. He hunts with the gun also."

"What does he do for money?"

"He sells some of what he grows and hunts. But he does not need so much in any case."

"Do many people live out there in the forest like that?" I asked.

"Oh yes", replied Carina, "Quite a number. Perhaps not so many as in the past."

I looked out the window at the falling snow, the trees still very heavily weighed-down by it all. The forest felt impenetrable.

I tried to imagine what it was like to live 'out there' somewhere, away from the road and with no electricity. I decided it must be incredibly quiet. And really quite beautiful.

And, as we walked back from the shop, it made Emma and I realise that although we had left a lot of noise and chaos behind in the UK, and that, for us, Sweden itself felt remote, quiet and wonderfully attractive, there were people for whom even this much peace and quiet was not enough. People like Farfarn who retired even further from all the trappings of modern life and still lived, quite happily, deep in the snow-covered forest. It seemed quite incredible.

We returned home to find a note pinned to our front door. It read "Hi, sorry I missed you. Called to see about your water problem. Will call back later. Around 6pm. Olof".

Our 'water problem' wasn't medical and Olof wasn't a doctor. He was the local plumber and during one of the recent exceptionally cold spells, where temperatures hadn't risen above -20 °C for four days, a pipe had burst in our cellar. It wasn't a major leak but it did seem to be affecting the pressure in the central heating boiler and if the pressure went too far awry, so we had been told, the boiler could pack up altogether. I could fix the odd dripping tap but this was something potentially more serious so we had asked around and been told that Olof was the man to see.

Good to his word, about 6.05 pm that same evening, headlights appeared on the drive and Olof soon emerged from his little red van clutching a tool-bag.

Although we had seen his vehicle coming along the drive, before we had had time to put on our boots and go out to meet him, Olof had already managed to skip up to our door and knock it. We opened the door, he said hello, we said hello back but before introductions had been made, Olof had kicked off his boots and sauntered into the house as if he was a regular visitor.

Olof was smaller than me – a fact that I was particularly proud of simply because, or so it seemed to me, every other man in Sweden was taller than I was. (Even though at six feet I was not small myself.) He was also on the rotund side and mostly bald. In fact he reminded me of a dwarven magician I had seen in a children's book many years beforehand, and it wouldn't have surprised either of us if he had produced a box of magic tricks and started doing some conjuring.

What Olof lacked in stature, however, he made up for in personality. And the evening began with his giving us a quick guided tour of the house, our own house, combined with a whole lot of information about who had lived here before, and what they had done, and what had been here in the distant past, and the adventures they had all had.

This short almost breathless tour de force culminated in the kitchen right by the kettle and coffee maker. And we all sat down for our first tea break.

Olof clearly enjoyed a cup of coffee, and a biscuit too. But he wasn't the kind to sit quietly and admire the thick snowflakes now landing heavily on the kitchen windowsill. And as soon as I mentioned how pretty they looked, he put his cup down and launched into another entertaining monologue about how much snow we could normally expect, and why, and how it had changed since his youth, and how ice wasn't always to be trusted and that the different kinds of snow meant, somehow, that it was important to call a plumber even if you didn't think you needed one.

I wish I had kept notes at the time as I was sure, afterwards, that some of the information would have come in very handy.

Teas and coffees finished, we got onto the subject of our water problem.

We told Olof what we thought the issue was, he nodded and we all stood up and headed for the door – as access to the cellar was from the outside. But before any of us had our boots on, there was a great rumble and crash right outside the door. And a mountainous pile of snow, which had chosen that moment to slide down off the roof, now blocked us in.

"That always seems to happen to me", said Olof peering out into the night. And with that he began telling us how, as a young man, his grandfather had once rescued an old couple from a house after they had been blocked in in just the same way. Overnight the snow had suddenly frozen and in the morning the ice was immovable. In the middle of nowhere with no other machinery handy, his grandfather had used his initiative and taken a chainsaw to the ice and cut through it in no time at all, the only problem being that the chainsaw also took away a good chunk of their front door too, as well as part of their wooden wall. He chuckled at the thought of this and then told us another tale about another relative who had fallen through ice and somehow pulled themselves ashore only to find a bear waiting for them.

"What happened", asked Emma.

"He jumped again into the water and managed to finally escape the other way. The bear obviously didn't want to get itself wet!"

Fortunately we also had a back door, so we went out through that and down to the cellar. Confronted by the leaking pipe, Olof was a different man. He worked hard and fast and quietly. Without a word and within minutes the job was done.

"There we are", he smiled. "Better than it was before." He silently put his tools carefully back into his tool bag, cleaning each as he did so, finished off and stood up straight.

"Do you know any jokes?" he asked and before we could answer he launched into a rapid-fire series of jokes. All in English. And all of which, or so it seemed to us, we remembered from our childhood.

This onslaught continued on the way back up from the cellar and throughout most of the next 30 minutes or so while we all had another cup of coffee.

Somehow we eventually managed to stop the flow of jokes and turned the conversation round to the village and some of the people who lived there. We talked about the shop, he told us about the church and how the roof leaked, we asked about the school and then we mentioned the old farmhouse on the far side of the village with all the broken fences and pigs.

Olof paused and smiled again. "That's me!" he said. "Those are my pigs."

Emma and I exchanged a brief glance. Although we didn't often go out of the village in that direction – there was nothing but forest that way for 50 miles – we had noticed the old farmhouse and had wondered who lived out there. It all looked quite chaotic. The pigs were big. And the fencing, or so it appeared to our eyes, was insufficient for the job of keeping them in one place.

Olof seemed to know what we were thinking, "Yes, that is my place. With the fences. Which are not so good. I know. But I never really seem to be at home long enough to fix them properly.

And my pigs are not bad animals and when they do get away they just go for a while, a little walk in the skog and then come back home."

"What do you do with them?" asked Emma somewhat naively.

"They get live a good life. They get big. They get fat. Then they go to the butcher", beamed Olof. He finished his drink in one gulp and stood up smartly. We assumed he was going to leave, instead, he launched into another joke which required him to perform some physical actions. It wasn't really any funnier than his others but he enjoyed himself and he clearly had a talent for performing that seemed to belie the notion that Swedes were standoffish and dignified. Another gag or two followed and then he said he had to go as he still had another couple of visits to make that evening.

As we all went out into the snow and the dark – by now it was about 9.30 pm – Olof stopped and looked at Emma. "Have you seen our calendar for next year?"

"No? Why?"

"Everyone from the village is in it. Sooner or later", Olof answered with a schoolboyish grin.

We were obviously missing something.

"Wait", he said, "I have one in my van. I will show you".

He disappeared into the back of his van and re-emerged after a moment or two carrying a copy of the calendar. He showed it to Emma. She blushed a little. Then he showed it to me. I turned the calendar around. Looked at it from different angles. "Is that Carina from the shop?" I finally asked.

"Yes", said Olof, that same grin getting a little broader.

I looked at the calendar that bit longer than I might otherwise have done.

"It was my idea", said Olof. "I do my pigs, I do my plumbing and I am also responsible for getting money for charity. So I had the idea one day to get people from the village to pose naked in the village calendar and sell it for charity". He looked at Emma. "They are not so naughty really, are they? Everything is hidden."

"Almost everything", she added laughing and, at the same time, taking the calendar out of my hands.

Olof laughed, too. "But it is men one year, of course. Women only the next. Each takes it in turns."

Later that evening we both checked out the calendars from previous years on the internet. They were all of the same genre. Quite decent really. Nothing crude. And all sold for charity. All the same, as I clicked on a few more photos of Carina, I couldn't help but remark, "It's funny how people look different without their clothes isn't it?"

*

Back in the UK, Emma and I had always spent a lot of time rummaging in charity shops. Charities like Oxfam, Barnardos and Help the Aged took over empty premises in the High Street and sold second hand goods like lamps, jigsaws, books and so on. The bigger ones often sold small items of furniture too. When we were younger we had both bought clothes from these shops. They had been a key part of our lives – at least in terms of shopping.

Visits to other European countries had taught us that these charity shops were pretty much a wholly British thing. There may have been the odd place in France selling second hand stuff, but there just weren't whole high streets filled with such places.

Why that was the case, we had no idea. Perhaps other Europeans had more expendable income and didn't need second hand goods, or perhaps the British had a more charitable streak. We didn't know the answer. But on the admittedly rare occasions that we were on holiday in Spain or wherever and giving charity shops and shopping any thought, we did miss them.

So it was to our surprise, and some delight, that we heard that charity shops existed – albeit in a different form – in Sweden.

We had first heard about them from Carina, the woman who worked in the local shop and interested all the local lumberjacks. Talking about nothing in particular, she mentioned "a wonderful shop full of almost everything. And not at all expensive".

It sounded interesting and we asked her what it was called. "Röda Korset. And all the money they make goes to good things."

Röda Korset was, of course, the Red Cross. And just as with charity shops in the UK, all the profits went to various charitable causes.

So on one comparatively warm and sunny February day, where the temperature climbed up to the dizzy heights of about 2 °C, Emma and I set off to discover the Swedish version of our beloved and sorely missed charity shop.

The Red Cross was situated in the nearby town of Växjö (a scary looking word pronounced Veck-Fur, Veck-Shur or, seemingly, in any one of a half dozen other different ways).

Veck-Fur – our preferred pronunciation – was an incredibly green town. Surrounded by lakes and almost invisible from the ring road because of the forest, the place had won several European awards for its low levels of pollution and innovative ideas in terms of energy saving. It wasn't massive in terms of population, but it did spread out over a largish area – there is no shortage of space in Sweden, after all – and so we expected our search for the charity shop to take a fair while.

In fact we found the Red Cross quite easily. Partly because it was signposted from the edge of town, but also partly because it was only open on two days a week and the crowds that flocked towards it were on a par with those you might find at a lower league football match.

Although, as we later discovered, high street charity shops as they are in the UK do exist in Sweden, this place was nothing like one of them; it was vast. A not-so-small warehouse full of all kinds of stuff at incredibly low prices. Prices reminiscent of the 1980s rather than the 2010s.

It was like Aladdin's cave. It was fantastic. There were unbelievable bargains to be found and we quickly wished we had brought a large van rather than our own small car.

There were genuine and working wooden spinning wheels for as little as the equivalent of £10. There were blanket chests with heavy iron hinges dating back to the 1800s for not much more. There was a good selection of those ghastly West German vases from the 1970s – some of which cost pence rather than pounds. There were genuine fur coats with posh Stockholm labels for a tenner. Leather coats too. There were countless hundreds of types of wooden ornaments and kitchen utensils.

Our particular favourites were two chaise-longues, horsehair filled and each costing about ten or twelve pounds. They were unbelievably comfortable.

There was also a small cafe in the warehouse. True, the coffee was weak as it seemed to be everywhere in Sweden, and the cakes were much too sugary, as they also seemed to be everywhere in

Sweden, but as the proceeds from the cafe went to charity, we bought some and took the opportunity to sit down for a little while before exploring the rest of the building.

As we sat and talked a very old chap, who was slowly shuffling past our table with a cup of coffee, stopped and asked us if we were English or American. We answered him and he asked if he could sit with us for five minutes to practice his English.

We of course said that we'd be happy for him to do so.

So he sat down. He must have been at least 80 years old, possibly older. And though he clearly had some mobility problems, he was still very upright and his eyes were bright and full of life.

As we talked he told us how Sweden "looked after everyone, the old, the young and especially children". He didn't say it as a boast, he just stated it in a quite matter of fact way. He told us there were no homeless, or rather that there had been none until the "new European countries" had joined the EU. He told us how winters had become so much shorter and easier than when he was young. He also told us how, when he was a young boy, he had heard the rumbling of guns and explosions in the distance, coming across the Baltic Sea from Germany in 1945.

I asked him if he ever remembered Sweden being at war. He laughed at this and said no. Sweden had not been a war since about 1815.

We ended the day, walking around the centre of Veck-Fur carrying a few bagful's of ornaments and clothes from the charity shop. Although it was cold, we sat down for a few minutes by the side of the main lake. The architecture in the city was functional and not all that attractive. But this was more than made up for by the beauty of the natural surroundings.

Once again there were people out on the ice playing hockey, walking dogs, skating and more besides. And not for the first time it struck us how wealthy a country Sweden really was. There just didn't seem to be any signs of poverty. And when people were down, the state seemed to be there to help them back up.

Of course in the three big cities of Stockholm, Gothenburg and Malmo, we knew there were some very large and pretty poor estates. There were some big problems with immigration there too. But all that felt a million miles away from smart green towns like Växjö.

Was that due to having not been in a war for two hundred years? Or was it down to a collective will to help one another? Something perhaps necessitated by the cold and often harsh climate? We didn't know. But although Sweden felt incredibly familiar to us at times, with its charity shops and cafes and everyone speaking English, it also felt very different to Britain in some ways too. It made us think that we had gone back to the UK of the 1950s. There was less rush. Less pressure. More space. And more security too.

March

Snow still lay thick on the ground, the trees, the rooftops and the pavements as March began. It was still just as pretty and everything was just as quiet. We liked that. More than that, we were positively enamoured of it. But being British and so unused to such long winters, we still felt the need to get away for a few days. To give ourselves some sort of reward for having survived a rural Swedish winter thus far.

In the end Emma hit on the idea of driving to Kalmar and spending a few days there.

Kalmar isn't a large city by British standards. It isn't a large city by any standards. In fact it isn't really a city at all. It is a town.

In truth there are only three real cities in the whole of Sweden; Stockholm, the capital with about 2 million people (a fifth of the total Swedish population), Gothenburg on the west coast with about half a million and Malmo down south with a population of about 200,000 or so. Everything else of any size is pretty much a large town rather than what we were used to calling a city.

Nevertheless, compared to our village and the all-encompassing silence of the deep winter, the prospect of spending a weekend in Kalmar felt – to us – on a par with winning an all-expenses paid trip to Las Vegas.

The pavements would probably be free of ice. There would be (some) large stores to look in, bright lights, places to sit and eat and maybe we would even go to a theatre or something.

True it wasn't going to be a break in the sun, but it would give us the chance to see somewhere new, and Kalmar was also supposed to be a very old and a very pretty town situated, as it was, on the Swedish coastline near the tourist island of Öland.

So yes, we decided we would go.

We booked a hotel in the centre, packed next to nothing in the car and set off – later than we'd planned, as it was beginning to get dark – to spend a weekend in those bright lights.

Even though it was only two hours' drive away, there was nothing between us and Kalmar except for a few villages and one very small town. The rest of the drive, along a very straight new road, was through forest. Unbroken forest.

At first the drive was fun. The miles slipped by. The road was almost empty and we thought that this was driving as God had intended it to be.

But after the umpteenth small hill revealed yet another long (long) stretch of modern empty road bordered by tall green spruce trees, and a harsh-looking wire fence designed to keep moose off the road, we decided to change tack and drive along the back roads.

After all, with no need to rush and our hotel already booked and paid for, it seemed a bit daft to rush along seeing nothing when there were old twisting winding lanes that we could follow instead. So we turned off at the very next junction, left modernity behind and began to drive through the forest itself.

The drive was extraordinarily pretty. Bordering on the theme park. And we discussed the idea of opening 'Snow World' in Sweden and becoming millionaires. There would be snow homes, wildlife tracking, swings and ropes in the treetops, coloured lights and midnight bonfires. And all that would be done in temperatures of minus 10 °C, with the nearest other humans being over an hour's drive away.

It was a superb idea. We both saw it clearly. Suddenly Sweden seemed to be a land of opportunity.

Then we noticed a few minor obstacles such as the lack of funds, a lack of roads, the lack of a nearby airport, no electricity, no internet, the fact that people might freeze to death – and so the superb idea was soon forgotten and we got back to focussing on the winter wonderland all around us and enjoying it in private.

Impressive as it was, the drive was also an uneventful one. Or at least it would have been uneventful except for the fact that, just as we neared Kalmar itself, a blizzard hit.

Blizzards were the kind of things that I used to read about in Boys' Own adventure comics when I was young. They would appear from nowhere and doom all but the bravest of souls to an early and unexpected end. Driving winds, sandstorms and tempests. It was the kind of weather that finished Scott and his party when they battled to get to and from the South Pole. It was the sort of weather that prevented mountaineers from coming back from the top of Mount Everest, their bodies to be found 50 years later preserved by the cold and ice.

Blizzards were that kind of thing. And I had never expected to meet one for real.

But this one *was* real. Very real.

A harsh, driving wind had made its horizontal way straight across from Siberia and had waited, somewhere out in the Baltic Sea, for us to get close enough to Kalmar so that we had started to imagine we could smell the restaurants and feel ourselves relaxing in a smart Swedish hotel with a glass or two of Absolut Vodka.

For a while, at first, as the storm hit, we soldiered on. The wind blew. The snow blew with it. And then the snow began to dance. It drifted and threw itself up in the air and came back down again in thin but opaque veils. It twirled around tree trunks and flicked long icy sprays at our windscreen. And the road, which had been more or less clear of snow, perhaps no more than a few centimetres deep, was suddenly lost under this new whirling white curtain. We could see nothing. Or almost nothing.

It should be mentioned at this point that, during October, plastic orange posts looking a little like skiing poles are placed along the length of pretty much every single road in Sweden. We had noticed these when buying our home. But we hadn't given any thought as to their purpose or to just how useful they could be.

Now, and quite suddenly, we could see both their purpose and their usefulness; the poles stood there, fluorescent beacons of hope, lit up by our headlights and showing us clearly where the edge of the road was – or would have been were it not for the snow – and so keeping us more or less on a straight and true course. And in no time at all we were very glad of such Swedish know-how.

"We'll be ok", I said, not fully believing my own words, "Just as long as we take it easy and stick between the orange posts".

And that was what we did. And it did work very well. At first. With those guiding poles and the windscreen wipers switching back and forth in an almost demented fashion and with our speed reduced to about 20 kph (that's about 15 miles an hour), we could just about see where the road was and so we pressed on.

"Kalmar can't be much further", said Emma with more than a little bit of wishful thinking in her words.

But then, as if in response to her brave optimism, the wind seemed to crank up another notch and, with what was surely a deliberate attempt to frustrate our plans, it started gusting the snow off the trees themselves as well. Great clumps of the stuff. Falling some metres in front of the car and then being rapidly dissipated by the wind to produce an even thicker curtain of the dancing, drifting, wild whiteness.

"It's no good, I'll have to stop or something", said Emma who was behind the wheel, "I can't see the road at all now. I can't even see the orange posts any more".

And nor could I.

So we came to a stop where we were, in the middle of the road, or so we assumed, and wondered how long we were going to be there. The road was quiet. In fact we hadn't seen a single vehicle for over half an hour.

"We're going to get snowed in", said Emma after a few minutes, "We're going to disappear under the snow like that blasted snow-blower and not be found until the spring!"

I could hear an edge of hysteria in her voice and so I said nothing – in case I had the same in my own voice.

For ten more minutes the wind blew. Blew, blasted and hammered. And we sat there, marooned, in our car watching swirls and whirls of white pitching and tossing against the dark backdrop of the forest. Wondering if we would still be alive by the thaw in April.

The snow was quickly building up around our car and we began to wish we had packed things like clothes, food, blankets, a thermos and rocket flares. Not the kind of thing you would normally need to consider when commuting round the M25 in England.

Then, thankfully, it stopped. As suddenly as it had begun.

Sudden. Stopped.

Still.

Silence.

The wind had gone. The snow stopped dancing. The orange posts re-appeared, we could see the road again – albeit now snow covered – and there was hope once more.

I doubt that anyone had ever been more relieved than we were to hear their own car start up again. And, even better, to start moving forward once more.

At first progress was slow, quite naturally, because in places the fresh snow had piled up against tree trunks and spilled over, in deep drifts, onto the road. Fortunately for us, we soon realised that this sort of snow was as soft as talcum powder and could be driven through easily.

Ten minutes more in the forest and a sharp left bend took us back onto the main road, illuminated hugely as it was by a double-trailered logging truck which was festooned with lights like a Christmas tree. These monsters, which shook the earth as they passed, were normally the kind of vehicles that made us wince. But on this occasion we were delighted to see it. It thundered past in the direction of the coast and we tucked our own car right behind it, slipstreamed along as far as Kalmar, once more feeling that we were not wholly alone in the wilderness.

*

Until it joined the EU in 1995, Sweden was a fairly closed and inaccessible country in a lot of ways. But the opening of the Öresund bridge – which connects the country to Denmark and so to the rest of Europe – has made quite a difference. And, in recent years, the population, which had been quite stable, has started to increase.

Danes and Germans, as well as a few Brits, are now taking advantage of the relatively low house prices and moving to southern Sweden. And, in turn, Sweden is slowly discovering new foods and new ideas in terms of shops and stores.

Kalmar was one city (or, rather, large town) which was benefitting from this new growth. Situated about 3 hours' drive from Copenhagen it had seen the arrival of a whole lot of new 'out of town' development. A relatively unknown phenomenon in this part of the world, these big stores gave Kalmar an unusual appearance for a Swedish town. To us, admittedly some of the names were more than familiar, such as IKEA, but there were also things like the huge German DIY store, Bauhaus. And – as we now lived in a tiny and remote village - we drove past these glowing storefronts envious of their offerings like two children with their faces pressed to a sweet shop window.

Our hotel, however, was in the old part of town. And no matter how much we wanted to stop and look at the bright lights of these big shiny new shops, they could wait until tomorrow. The blizzard had made us late, we felt tired and probably a bit stressed from the experience and so we drove straight past this new, and clearly thriving, part of Kalmar and headed for our hotel instead.

Situated just a few hundred yards from the grand old castle on the Kalmar coast, we found our hotel easily enough. The castle itself look stunning, with copper domes and seemingly moated, it was like something out of a dream. But once again – due to hunger and being tired – we put off any lingering over such sites.

The staff at the hotel were efficient and friendly and we were soon in our room. Like all Swedish hotels, this one was pretty expensive but it made up for that by being very comfortable.

I think both of us could have just gone straight to bed. But a quick shower woke me up, a strong coffee did the same for Emma and, as we were only here for two nights, we summoned up the enthusiasm to change and set off to experience our first Swedish restaurant.

We had read some reviews – written by Swedish people – of some restaurants in Kalmar and they all seemed to be pretty good. Not content with that we had asked around in our village and Carina had also told us that there was a particularly good restaurant quite near to the castle. And as the castle was easy to find, that was the place we made for.

We arrived at the restaurant about 7.30 pm. It was a smart looking place with a spacious car park half full of Volvos and expensive BMWs, Quite dimly lit but in a comfortable and inviting sort of way. There also seemed to be a good number of people both inside eating and just arriving as we did.

"Looks ideal", said Emma.

With hindsight, I should have suspected something as soon as we walked through the doors. I had spent a year or two in France, when I was younger, working in a variety of jobs and often eating in restaurants. Back then I had learned, or perhaps it was more a basic sort of survival instinct, that if a restaurant didn't smell of good food, it wouldn't serve good food. I had even gotten pretty good at walking in and then walking out of a place if it didn't have that home-cooked, fresh food feel to it.

Sadly that was back then, in France, and for some reason I had clearly forgotten those lessons upon arriving in Sweden.

We were soon seated and the menu quickly arrived. We studied it for a while and then looked at each other. If I was generous, I suppose it could have been described as eclectic if nothing else. Experimental, even. It certainly didn't seem to offer the traditional Scandinavian food we were rather hoping for.

"Curry sauce with basil?" I said. I was used to curry sauce. But I had never seen it served with basil.

"And with salmon. And with cream", said Emma.

"The cream is optional", I noticed.

It didn't look promising. But, well, we were here. We had driven far enough. And we were hungry. And, to be honest, the numerous kebab and pizza restaurants we had already driven past in Kalmar didn't look any better either. So we ordered and sat back enjoying the expensive feel of the restaurant and the politely quiet hum of conversation going on around us.

It all felt rather nice. Scandinavian chic.

And then the starter arrived.

The starter was supposed to be seafood. And it might have been. Once. A very long time ago. But that was probably back when

Sweden was still under ice around 10,000 years ago. And by now it was much closer to fossil rather than seafood. After toying with it for a few minutes, we both pushed the inedible stuff to the side of the plate.

It did come served with a sauce. And a salad. Or, rather, it did come served with a packet sauce that still had powder in it and a few leaves of lettuce that looked like they had been run over several times in the car park.

We wondered. Was it just us? Were we being tested? Had they spotted us as 'foreign' and decided to give us last week's leftovers?

We looked around at the other diners.

They almost all appeared to be tucking in happily. Smart Swedish businessmen and women. The odd presumably local family. A single man or woman here or there using a tablet at the same time as eating. All healthy looking. All Scandinavian, as far as we could tell.

Still in the absence of the healthy smell of cooking, although with the odd ping in the distance as the microwave announced itself ready, the debris of our starter was taken away and the main course soon arrived.

By now we had the firm suspicion that this wasn't really a good restaurant. It did have good reviews both on the internet and from Carina. But clearly something somewhere was wrong.

As to the main course, Emma had three kinds of sill (herring) with potatoes. A famous Scandinavian dish. And I had salmon, also with potatoes. True, that meant that both courses were fish, but that hadn't seemed a problem when we ordered. After all, we were by the coast and wanted to eat fresh fish on our first night out. I had eaten seafood followed by fish many times in France.

As it turned out both choices were a mistake.

The sill – a pickled herring prepared in a variety of ways – turned out to be mainly sugar and dill. There were good-sized pieces of fish too, but those other two ingredients had been so totally overdone that there was nothing to be tasted except sugar and dill. Which, horrid as it was, at least partially concealed the fact that the fish was stale.

The potatoes had also been cooked in dill. And the rather sad salad also had a few sprigs of dill.

Emma looked around for the 'Dill Week' signs but, alas, there were none. This was standard fare.

My potatoes were the same. Dilly. And my salmon had also suffered a similar fate. It tasted of dill and, faintly, sugar. But I did have one advantage, my salmon was also smoked. In fact it was more than smoked. It tasted well off. Old. In fact it tasted more like it had been smoking 60 a day for most of a very long life before it finally succumbed to an overdose of dill.

Needless to say the dessert was much the same. Sugar, with a little extra sugar for good measure and a thin wet sauce which was rather depressing and resembled a smudge of melted snow.

Of course a dessert should be sweet. But. Somehow... Not like this.

As with Emma's main course, none of the sweetness seemed to be fresh or exciting or hinted it or just suggested. It all seemed to be ladled on. Cheap white sugar, by the bucket full. The kind of sweetness we both remembered from visiting our respective grandparents in the 1970s, on Sunday afternoons, whilst absent-mindedly spooning too much Tate and Lyle into milky tea and dunking cheap digestive biscuits into the resulting sugar soup.

It was over the top. And out of date. Like a meal from the 1970s. Or even the 1950s.

We finished off with a coffee – surprisingly decent and the first time we had had a good one in Sweden – and looked around the room for signs of disgust or even disbelief on the faces of fellow guests. There were no such signs. Quite the opposite; people seemed happy. Content even.

As we paid and left, disputing whether or not to make a fuss but being, frankly, too timid to do so, we half wondered whether all the other diners were actually paid to sit there and look like they were enjoying themselves, the idea being to entice the odd unsuspecting outsider into the place. But no, there were too many of them, and their chatter and actions seemed too genuine.

Needless to say we were glad to leave. And we made a very definite mental note not to visit another restaurant without checking the menu in advance.

Only later did we realise that the fault did not lie with that particular restaurant...

The following morning, we had a breakfast in the hotel which almost – almost, but not quite – made up for the restaurant the night before. A huge open buffet style breakfast consisted of organic muesli with all sorts of extra ingredients to be added at will, local (and quite delicious) yoghurt, orange juice, sourdough bread and much more besides. It even featured a few varieties of sill. But just one quick taste of this proved that the restaurant had been no accident: the fish was stale, and all we could taste was sugar and dill.

Still, the rest of the breakfast was substantial and by the time we left the hotel to explore Kalmar and its environs, we were well enough fed to keep going for several hours.

Immediately adjacent to Kalmar, just a few kilometres across the water, lay the island of Öland. We had heard of the place only recently in a news item, on Swedish television, and apparently it was the place where the Swedish royal family liked to spend most of their time. Although probably not, to be fair, during winter.

50 km long but only a few kilometres wide, and once only accessible by ferry, Öland was now connected to the mainland of Sweden by a worryingly high bridge. And as we drove across it, I think both of us made a point of looking straight ahead and talking quite determinedly about something – anything! – other than bridges, water and heights.

Once on the other side, the landscape changed quite noticeably. Suddenly the world was very flat, very low lying and, seemingly, shut. Bars, restaurants, a marina and more besides, Öland had the feel of a vacation destination, a holiday island frozen (quite literally!) and waiting for summer to bring it back to life.

A small kiosk, selling desultory hot dogs which seemed to be ubiquitous throughout Sweden, was almost the only place we found that was open. We stopped for a coffee, listened to strange calls of sea birds – the names of which we didn't know - and then drove further into the island, seeing few signs of human life as we did so.

With the island only a few kilometres wide, we soon found ourselves on the east coast. Nothing but the Baltic between ourselves and Russia. Or perhaps Lithuania.

We got out of the car and walked to the water's edge.

To us this was a very unusual world.

The land we stood on appeared to be almost concrete – but it was not concrete, it was natural rock. Flat. hard. Grey. With just a sprinkling of tough grass for company. Much of the island appeared to be like that. Hard flat rock just underneath a few inches of soil.

The coast, too, was unusual or, at least, very different, from the coast we knew back in the UK. Here the water lapped, tideless, against grass. It would have been perfectly possible to drive one of those sit-on lawnmowers straight into the sea, and not even notice a bump between the land and the water.

Not only that, but the water was almost salt free. Cold. Icy even. You could have poured it straight into a vodka and drunk it without realising that it was seawater rather than tap water in the glass.

Still without sight or sound of any person – except for the distant rumble of an ancient looking tractor – we walked around a motley collection of wooden huts, weathered to within an inch of their lives and all painted Falun red. With odd posts and plastic buckets and nets and so on strung between them. We weren't sure what the huts and stuff were all for, it had the appearance of being from a computer game. A mysterious world that resembled Earth but which was subtly different, depopulated and cold.

Clearly Öland was a place that came to life as the seasons changed. Or perhaps we had just visited on a national holiday.

Despite the lack of pretty much anything, the peace on the island was wonderful. And with a pale thin blue sky overhead, and a weak weak sun, it almost felt idyllic.

Back in Kalmar – a town which had struck us as surprisingly quiet, clean and traffic free before our trip to the Baltic and which now seemed crowded and boisterous – we spent a few hours looking around shops and admiring the pastel coloured buildings which were such a feature of the 'old part' of Swedish towns. A cafe which made its own bread served decent and filling sandwiches, and we discovered a new take on cheesecake that was both good, slightly sour, and very filling.

On our second evening in Kalmar, possibly as a result of the meal the night before, but also perhaps because we were both quite tired from being out all day, we ate a fairly simple meal from the bar of the hotel itself. It wasn't exciting, but nor was it the kind of stuff you might have bad dreams about later.

The following morning, with Emma keen to get back to work and both of us feeling we had had a break (and wanting to get back to our own kitchen) we left Kalmar promising to visit it again. The town had character. It was clean, calm and pleasant. And there were numerous interesting looking shops. Small ones as well as the big chain stores. I loved browsing in antique shops, and we had even spotted a few of those the evening before whilst taking a quiet stroll through town under dark and frosty skies.

The castle itself, once open, had to be worth a visit, too. And we would definitely make another trip or two across to Öland. And perhaps next time, that too would be open.

*

With our visit to Kalmar already receding into the past, but the winter still very much in the present, I still had the distinct impression that I must have been missing out on 'key things to do in Sweden' during months of heavy snow.

Emma had recently begun work from home, via the internet. And so, financially, we were already finding our feet in Sweden. But if were to make a success of being here, and given that a large part of every year was clearly going to be spent under a thick white carpet of snow, I, too, needed to find a way of whiling away a few more of the winter hours.

"They must be doing something", I mused out loud one afternoon.

"Who?" Emma asked. I had just made her a coffee and she had taken a short break from her work.

"Them. The Swedish", I replied. "They can't all be buried inside their homes, like hibernating animals. Waiting for summer. And yet, really, we hardly ever see any sign of anyone".

Emma nodded. "They all take a break, at this time of year. From what I gather. A few weeks out to somewhere like Thailand".

I glanced up at the dark grey sky. I didn't blame them. For the last ten days or so I had forgotten what the sun looked like. It hadn't appeared once. Not even for ten minutes. I could see the appeal of Thailand.

"And others go to the mountains", she said, finishing her drink.

"Do they?" I asked, absent-mindedly, adding "Are they really that keen on climbing, then?"

Emma laughed. "Not for climbing. Skiing. Especially the younger ones".

Of course.

Why hadn't I thought of that?

Sweden was always winning gold medals in the Winter Olympics for skiing and suchlike. Winter sports must be a huge pastime. Perhaps that was what they were all doing? When not at work, they were off in the woods doing stuff like skating and skiing.

And so that afternoon I spent an hour or two researching winter sports. About which, prior to my studies, I knew nothing.

Sweden, it turned out, was a world leader in the sport of Nordic skiing. Otherwise known as cross-country skiing. And this was no accidental or chance event. The country was – for the most part – pretty flat. And yet it was also, as I could see for myself, covered with snow. For many months of the year. Today, it was true, snow could be shovelled out of the way with big yellow machines, or people could cross it with Ski Doos. But traditionally, snow was crossed on foot. Or, rather, snow covered land was crossed by feet attached to skis.

And, by all accounts, it was an extremely energetic and health giving sport.

As things would have it, only two days later I encountered skis myself. I had towed a trailer full of rubbish to the local recycling plant. Swedes are very big on recycling. And even in the depths of winter, it was still considered quite normal to ferry scrap and waste back and forth to the recycling facilities on the edge of Växjö. It didn't matter that was inconvenient, it didn't matter that it was -10 °C, the environment came first. Or civic pride came first, or a sense of shame, I wasn't sure. But the end result was the same. We all recycled.

One of the great advantages of this collective 'greenism' was that each recycling plant also housed a large shop. Large and cheap. Large and cheap and selling just about everything that could be pulled out of the waste containers and re-used. Somewhere. By someone.

I loved visiting this shop. It was – incredibly – even cheaper to buy stuff in there, than the Red Cross. Big wooden picture frames, for example, cost the equivalent of pennies. China and glass and even pewter items were almost given away.

So before leaving, and after having deposited my rubbish in the correct bins, where a young girl with almost white hair told me all about the history of the recycling plant – in near perfect English – I decided to pay a quick visit to the shop.

And there, at the door, outside the shop and before I had even begun to examine the pewter and picture frames, I saw them: skis. All sorts and shapes and sizes.

The problem was, for me, that I had no idea what sized ski I took. In boots I was a size 44. About 10 or so in UK terms. But how did that transfer to skis? Nor did I know what type of ski worked best in the forest. Some of them were very long and broad and I figured that those were probably 'Alpine' skis – the sort that whizz down mountains at horrendous speeds and give amateurs a broken leg. But there were some very narrow and comparatively short ones too. Some were even made of wood.

To be honest, I could have bought all of them for less than 50 GBP. And perhaps set up as an online ski salesman. There were dozens of the things. But I didn't want to go back home with the trailer more full of stuff than when I left. So just one pair would have to suffice.

The man in the shop – who also spoke very good English – turned out to be Greek and didn't know anything at all skis or skiing. But he directed me to the same platinum haired girl I had spoken to earlier. She, Gunnel, was apparently a local and upcoming star in the skiing world. She would be able to help.

And so it was that I arrived back home clutching a pair of skis which were shorter and wider than I had expected them to be. But which were, so Gunnel had assured me, ideal for skiing in forest on loose powder snow. (I had no real idea what loose powder snow was, but Gunnel was certain that it was the kind of stuff I would encounter and so I took her word for it.)

I ran up the steps to our door – we had two external doors, one of them being up a flight of steps and the other at ground level and currently buried under a couple of metres of snow – flung it open and called for Emma.

"Come on!" I shouted when I finally heard an inquiring noise from deep inside the house.

Emma appeared, warm in a grey jumper, and looking as if she had spent the last two hours asleep on one of the chaise-longues we had bought from the Red Cross. Which, she told me later, was exactly what she had been doing.

We already had a small plastic sledge. In bright orange, the colour of choice for snow, it seemed. And Emma brought that with her as we headed for the gently sloping range of hills to the rear of our house.

"Are you sure you know what you're doing?" she asked, looking doubtfully at my skis.

I nodded. "The girl who sold me these is some sort of skiing expert. She said that these would be ideal for a beginner".

Before arriving in Sweden, Emma and I had spent several hundred pounds on specialised winter clothing. Goggles, boots, quilted trousers and jackets. And today, with a wind howling down from the frozen wastes of goodness knew where, we were both very glad we had done so.

The hill wasn't long. Nor was it very high. But climbing up it in that wind, with the temperature down in the very low end of things, was pretty hard work. And we were relieved to finally reach the top where we paused for a short while for breath.

"Go on then", said Emma. Nodding at the skis. "Put them on and have a go".

"How?" We both looked at the skis.

Neither of us had any idea how to 'put a ski on'. And I hadn't even thought to ask Gunnel about it.

We puzzled over the fittings and fixtures for a few minutes. And neither of us could see any obvious way of attaching a boot (and so a foot!) to the ski.

And as the wind blew harder and we got colder, and the light began to fade, I realised that I was not about to discover a previously unknown talent. My skiing days were going to be pretty limited. At least for this winter.

Finally Emma – on her 50p orange plastic sledge – decided it was time to go. And with one small push from me, she shot off down the snow-covered slope and disappeared into the distance.

As for me, I had to trudge all the way back to the house carrying the blasted skis.

I felt very sheepish making my way back home without even having had a tiny go at skiing. But at the very moment when I crossed the road, a car passed and slowed down. It was Olof. Our plumber. He waved and I waved back.

And for all the world, it looked as if I had just spent an afternoon skiing out in the forest. And as I put my skis away in the cellar, I wondered how long it would be before Carina in the shop asked me how many years I had been a cross-country skier...

*

On the last Saturday of March, we awoke to a strange sight and a strange sound.

For a start the sun was shining. We had hardly seen it for the last two or three months. Indeed so dark was it, so often, that for a while we had wondered if the Arctic Circle had somehow slipped further south and, just like in the north of Sweden, we were actually having Arctic night. (Arctic night is the downside of the midnight sun. In northern Sweden, during summer, the sun never sets. That's the midnight sun. Gloomily, in winter, it does the reverse and never rises. For some months each year, in those northern parts, the only way you can tell if it is 'day' or 'night' is by looking at your watch! That's the Arctic night).

Of course it wasn't actually quite that dark. The sun was up. Somewhere. It was just that it never managed – barring the odd hour – to appear from behind the thick blanket of cloud and over the top of the trees at one and the same time.

Suddenly, however, it *had* done so. The sun was out and it looked and felt glorious. The sky seemed bluer than it ever used to back in the UK. And so unused to sunlight had we become that it actually hurt our eyes. In fact the light was so bright, the whole sensation so wonderful, that we could suddenly understand why, when skiing, people need to wear those thick red tinted goggles.

We stood and blinked at the sunlit day for a while, before it slowly dawned on us that something else had changed too.

Or at least was in the process of changing.

It wasn't just that the sun was out and the sky a deep clear blue, it was the snow.

The snow. It was going. Not gone. But going. The thaw was definitely happening.

In a way, once we realised this, it made us feel rather sad. Seeing the snow go was like losing a close friend. It had been with us for days. Weeks. Months even. And we had gotten used to the feel, sight, sounds and even smell of it. The world looked tidy when it was covered with a thick covering of snow. Without the snow it looked – or was starting to look – very untidy as bare branches and scrubby grass started to emerge once more.

Soon, signs of the thaw were everywhere.

A small river – normally a small river – borders our land. It has the odd trout in but, sadly, we aren't allowed to fish in it as the river has a special conservation status. Suddenly, however, it wasn't a small river. It was a white water torrent. The levels rose and rose as the snow melted all around it and further upstream and we worried for a while that the thing would burst its banks. Fortunately it didn't get quite that high. But the noise and power of the now raging stream was a sight to see.

"Surely we ought to be allowed to put some sort of wheel in there", I suggested one day, "You know, to generate electricity. It's absolutely hammering past at the moment and a water wheel would save us a fortune!"

"We're not really using that much electricity", said Emma. Which was true. It had been surprisingly cheap to heat and run our house in so many weeks of sub-zero temperatures.

"Perhaps we could store the energy and sell it?" I said. But the idea was soon forgotten. Generating our own electricity and making money from a surplus of the stuff sounded a good idea. But the required engineering was certainly way beyond my skills.

The thaw also made us think of Narnia where the white queen held the country under permanent winter until the royal lion set it free again.

And though the promise of oncoming spring was greater than I had ever known before, other signs of the thaw were less attractive.

Suddenly the roads were covered in slush. Oh dear. And we were reminded of why it was that, back in the UK, we hadn't been so keen to see or drive in snow. When it melts and becomes an ugly grey mush, it doesn't have much to offer.

Of course in Sweden, though it might melt once or twice early on in winter, generally speaking once the snow is down it stays down. Especially in the north. The reason for this is that, surprisingly perhaps, Sweden is actually a very dry country. And what moisture there is, in winter, comes down as – yes – more snow. It doesn't melt when the temperatures rise either, but that's mainly because, until the end of March at least, the temperatures just don't rise.

In the end, although we missed the silence of the snow and the brightness, once it had begun to melt it lost most of its attraction and we were glad to see the back of it.

And one week later, on exactly March 31st, it had all gone. We wondered if it was this punctual every year.

April

The first of April. And with the thaw we were pleased that spring had arrived at last.

Only it hadn't arrived. Not really.

The last sunny week in March combined with the thaw had filled us with the false belief that the winter was over and that the daffodils and crocuses would soon be out in flower. We even began to look forward to seeing the birds come back from their migrations south and to getting out into the garden and sowing some seeds in the vegetable beds. And on one particularly optimistic day we even talked about ice cream.

The first week of April taught us that we were wrong. Winter wasn't yet ready to throw in the towel.

To be fair, our misguided optimism was understandable. After all we were British and used to the British seasons, so of course winter should have finished at the end of March. If not sooner. In a good year, back in the UK, it could be mild and sunny at Easter, even if Easter fell in March.

But this wasn't a good year. And this wasn't the UK.

To begin with, we peered out of the window in turns and almost religiously, to see if our little thermometer was showing any signs of life. It wasn't. The temperature remained just above freezing and, on some nights, dropped down well below it.

"Perhaps it's broken", said Emma.

It wasn't. I knew that because we now had a big thermometer too and that told the same chilly story.

I should add at this point that I wasn't obsessed with the temperature. I didn't have two thermometers because I saw myself as some sort of amateur weatherman. In fact, by Swedish standards, I was a positive laggard in terms of my thermometer count. Edvard, our neighbour, had at least four. And by all accounts one chap in the village had six or more – some of which were very ornate and quite large. But even that was as nothing. Not really. Not in meteorological terms. Other neighbours had their own rain gauges. One or two even had little weather stations all of their own.

The exact reason for all these pieces of weather divining equipment was never wholly clear to us but, after being in Sweden just a short while, we had soon appreciated that the climate was harsh and that winter evenings could be long and dull. And from that it seemed somehow to follow that many men – it was never, surely, a woman – whiled away their spare time on those long nights compiling statistics about snow depth, sunshine hours and humidity.

By contrast we had ended up with two thermometers simply because one – the little one by the window – came with the house. And the second was an irresistible bargain at the nearby garden centre.

So. Anyway. We'd had two days, in that fast receding week of March, where the temperature had reached 10 °C. And now, in early April, we looked back on those days as distant and balmy. Almost tropical. Something out of a dream. But just as we were becoming resigned to what we hoped would be a minor setback in terms of the weather, the really bad news arrived.

One morning Edvard came over to our house to ask if the postman had left a parcel for him with us. We invited him in for a cup of tea, partly because he looked a little cold and fed up, but also because we wanted to interrogate him about the spring or, rather, the lack of it.

In the UK there are slots in every front door for delivery of the morning post. They are called letterboxes. And back in the old days – by which I mean the 1980s – even small packets and parcels would frequently be force-fed through these narrow slots as the postman tried his or her hardest to make a delivery on time. Admittedly this was often done to the detriment of the aforementioned packet or parcel, but at least we knew the post office had tried.

Those days may well be over now in the UK. But such days had never existed in Sweden. Because in Sweden there is no such thing as a letterbox. Not of that type. And certainly not in the countryside.

Instead, houses have an actual box, a bit like a bread bin, with a lid, which is fixed to a post at the end of your garden path, or even the end of your drive as the case may be. A box. For letters. For some of the more remote homes this can mean that their post is actually delivered to the end of a lane, as much as maybe 1 km or more from the house, and it often stands there in company with a half dozen other boxes belonging to other homes somewhere out there in the *skog*.

It is possible to buy one of these letterboxes which locks. But most don't lock. So this means that your post is in your letterbox, unsecured and maybe half a mile from your house, often for many hours in a day until you get back home from work.

Despite that, nothing – as far as we can tell – ever goes missing. At least nothing ever goes missing from the letterbox.

Sadly, just like in Britain, the Swedish post office still occasionally ends up sending stuff to the wrong house or even the wrong country and that, Edvard told us, was partly what he was worried about. His son had sent him something in a parcel. Quite a few weeks back. Edvard had had notification of delivery but he hadn't yet received anything. Ordinarily, he told us, the parcel would have been left in his letterbox or, if too large for the box itself, delivered to the village shop instead. That was normal enough. The problem was that when Edvard went to the shop to collect it, the parcel wasn't there. It hadn't been stolen. It just hadn't been delivered there. So he wondered if the postman had delivered it to us for safekeeping and he wanted to ask us to keep an eye out for it.

The three of us sat there for a while and talked about the post. We told Edvard that we were sure his parcel would turn up. And we assured him we would also ask about it if and when the postman next knocked at our door.

He cheered up a little. We chatted about one or two other things and then I took my chance to turn the conversation around to my current pet concern.

"So, is spring a little late this year?", I asked Edvard.

An expression of puzzlement crossed his fine Scandinavian brow. Edvard was probably over 80 years of age but he was still, very much, a handsome man in full possession of all his faculties. "Spring?"

"Yes", I continued, "It's the 7th of April now and the temperature is still very low. It will be Easter soon".

Edvard shook his head. "No. No. No. This is quite normal for April. Some years it may be a little warmer. Some years a little colder".

"When do the flowers start to come up?" Emma asked.

"Spring arrives during May", said Edvard firmly and with a hint of puzzlement in his voice, "Everything will grow then. It has always been like that".

Emma and I looked at each other. May? We were used to spring making an appearance in March and being in full flow by mid-April. We wouldn't know what to make of snowdrops in May and daffodils in June.

"I remember one year", continued Edvard, "when it snowed all the way through May. Even on the first of June we were still able to sledge down..."

I made my excuses and went outside to check my thermometers again.

*

As a child I had grown up in a big city and, like most other city kids, I had only a limited exposure to any wildlife. We had pets. Sometimes we visited the zoo in the school holidays. From train windows, we saw cows and sheep. And as if that vast quantity of wildlife wasn't enough, there was even an odd distant glimpse of a grey squirrel or reports of a fox being seen in a nearby field.

The more adventurous of our parents would hang up little red mesh bags stuffed with peanuts at some point in the garden. And that meant seeing such exotic species as the blue tit or even, once, in my case, a woodpecker. It landed on the net bag. Took a peck or two. The bag fell to the floor and the bird was off.

Sweden, in terms of wildlife, was very different.

For a start there were birds the size of small cars. Neither Emma nor I knew much about birds and we watched with awe as these great vulture-like things drifted lazily overhead or sometimes dive-bombed the ground in search of prey.

We researched them a little, Googled them, and we found that they were, mostly, buzzards, not eagles or condors. But they still looked every inch eagles to our untutored eyes and we wondered how they survived in the cold and the snow when, presumably, most of their prey was under that snow and safely out of sight and it must often have taken them hours to find the smallest of snacks.

Further south in Sweden, perhaps an hour or so from us, in the county of Skåne or Scania, deer were also present in abundance. Not just the odd animal here or there timidly sneaking across the road and being startled by headlights – but small armies of them crossing roads in lines and often holding the traffic up, only to disappear rapidly into trees or fields again. For all we knew there were such herds of deer in Kronoberg too. But the forest was so thick and so vast that around us, we assumed, they had no need to show their faces very often.

One animal we had never encountered, but had heard a lot about, was the wild boar. By all accounts there were tens of thousands of them at large in the *skog* and, when approached, depending on their mood, they could get quite nasty. At least that was what our neighbour Edvard told us. And as he was a keen hunter, we had no reason to disbelieve him and go in search of a boar to upset.

It was true that bear and wolves existed in good numbers too. But they were – sadly or thankfully depending on your viewpoint – some long way north of where we lived. As was the giant weasel known as the wolverine.

Then there was the lynx, Europe's last surviving big cat. They did live in the skog, even in Kronoberg. But, again according to Edvard, although capable of eviscerating a human with one swipe of the paw, they were shy, gentle and extremely hard to see. And far more likely to run away than stand and fight. So, after our initial concerns, we didn't spend too much time worrying about meeting one of those either.

Indeed apart from odd strange tracks, initially in the snow but now in the mud, we saw none of these particular animals. None of the wildlife.

Not for a while anyway.

That changed on one fine April day when I was working in the garden.

Moose are big. Bigger than horses. Awkward in gait, covered in shaggy brown fur and rather strange looking with long lugubrious faces, they are at one and the same time both graceful and slightly comical. They also have knees which seem to bend the wrong way – talking to Edvard about this later, I discovered that this is to allow them to cross the otherwise impenetrable *skog*, a skill which they possess to a far greater level than any other animal.

In addition to all of this the moose is probably also the subject of more stories in Sweden than every other animal combined.

For a start we had heard stories about moose getting drunk. Apparently they adore eating apples. The apples ferment slowly in their stomachs. And the alcohol produced intoxicates the moose.

We didn't quite understand or believe the biology and chemistry involved in this process, but when we read in the newspaper of the emergency services being called out to rescue a drunken moose, it became clear to us that this was indeed something that could happen. (The particular story was that a moose had reached up into someone's apple tree, in their garden, to get the very highest apples. Being already the worse for wear – drunk – it had lost its balance and somehow gotten stuck on the tree trunk. The owner had heard the animal bellowing angrily and gone out into his garden to see what the fuss was about. He had tried to approach the moose but soon saw that it was inebriated. So he had called the fire brigade. The story had a happy ending. The moose was sedated and released from the tree. The owner of the tree wasn't at all bothered about losing one of his apple trees and cared more that the moose was alright.)

There were other strange stories about moose too. According to these reports, it was the moose, and not the bear nor the wolf, not even the boar, that was the most dangerous of all Swedish wildlife.

Once again we found this hard to believe. We couldn't imagine a deer-like animal being more of a threat than an angry bear. But yet again, there was confirmation from time to time in the newspapers, some of it quite gory.

All the same, I had yet to meet one of these uniquely northern animals in the flesh.

But that was about to change..

Winter was finally over. The sun was out. It was mild but not warm. And the sky was a beautiful blue, the same colour as the Swedish flag.

I was busy in the garden cutting a few broken and lop-sided branches off our apple trees. They had been quite badly mangled by some heavy snow back in March, and although it was a first for me to do real pruning – and albeit my work was a little haphazard and probably being done at totally the wrong time of year – I was quite enjoying myself.

Every now and then my pile of broken and sawn twigs and branches got a little out of hand and so I stopped work to collect them up and take them over to the house. The idea was that, at some point in the future, I would stack them all and dry them for feeding to our wood-burning stove.

I was strolling back from one of these little trips – from the house and heading back to the apple trees – when I saw the moose.

Where exactly he or she had emerged from the *skog*, I couldn't say. But by the time I noticed the creature, it was no more than 10 metres away from me and right in the middle of my garden.

Antlers and all.

At first, once I realised that there was a large wild animal so close, I thought I ought to run away. But I quickly figured that it was going to be able to cross the land much faster than I could. So I stayed, stock still, just where I was, vaguely remembering some advice about doing that if ever confronted by a bear.

Oddly, the moose too was quite surprised to see me. Possibly more shocked than I was. Our house had been empty for a few years before we purchased it, and in all likelihood, the moose had crossed the land many times in recent years and never met a soul.

It, too, stopped.

And the thought crossed my mind, as we watched one another, that perhaps it had heard the same advice about bears and keeping still that I had heard.

Then it looked straight at me. Flared its nostrils.

This was my moment, I thought to myself. My time was up. It was sure to decide that any battle between us would be short and sweet and it would be the victor.

But no. It just stood there. Nose twitching a little.

We watched one another for what seemed a very long time. But which was, in truth, probably no more than 30 seconds or so.

It would be wrong of me to call it a handsome animal. Because it wasn't. If anything it resembled a camel – but a camel in dark brown fur and without a hump. But there was a 'niceness' to its face that camels don't really have. And I was impressed by its camouflage too; by how such a large beast had gotten so close to me before I had noticed it, without making a sound.

Suddenly the moose made a clear decision. Visibly, the expression on its face changed. It decided that I was just not worth worrying about. It wasn't going to charge me, head down. I wasn't a threat. And it could just carry on strolling across my garden. And that was precisely what it did do. Sort of running, sort of walking, sort of hobbling, the moose sniffed and went on its way. Crossing the lawn as if I wasn't there. It didn't run any faster. It didn't run from me. It didn't even turn to look back at me. In fact, for all the world, I got the distinct impression that it probably sighed to itself and thought something like, "Oh damn. Someone's bought the old house. From now on I suppose I'll have to go the long way around".

Soon enough my first moose was gone.

And with that I scuttled back into the house and told Emma all about it.

Naturally she didn't believe me. But her own close encounter with a moose was no more than 48 hours away...

Emma had studied archaeology at university. We had met there, in Wales. I was more or less interested in anything and everything. So, together, it was quite natural that we had often visited heritage sites or places with interesting legends and so forth in the UK and even in France on our holidays there.

Sweden was completely new to both of us in that respect. I knew virtually nothing of its history beyond the fact that it no longer got involved in wars, had once been very powerful (albeit for a short period of time) and that the king sometimes rode a bicycle through the streets of Stockholm.

Emma, too, had only just begun to discover its archaeology. But one cloudless morning, just two days after my moose encounter, she enthusiastically took us out for a day trip to visit some 'local' sites of interest which she had been reading about on the internet.

As might be expected in such a large and relatively empty country, traffic levels are light in Sweden and driving is usually a pleasure. (Except during blizzards!) These days there are probably more cars on the average English country lane than there are on what passes for a motorway in Sweden.

Many back roads, through the Swedish *skog*, are not tarmacked at all, but are made of a kind of hard clay mixed with gravel. And despite the many thousands of miles of such roads, potholes are soon filled, even on lanes that can barely see more than one car an hour.

Emma preferred the tarmac. She had spent several years commuting in the UK and had spent quite a lot of those years sitting in traffic jams. There were none of these in Sweden. At least there were none away from the big three cities. And so for her, to drive on good straight and almost empty roads was quite a treat.

I particularly enjoyed driving on the clay lanes in the forest. They would often wind for miles – quite literally – before another car or house would come into view. And the dark forest often parted to give an unexpected glimpse of meadow or a lake or something else.

Rather like Jack Spratt and his wife, the combination worked very well for us. Sweden is a big country and so "local" can mean anything up to 100 km away. And in the north of Sweden, 200 km is considered a neighbour. So Emma would drive the long straight roads, with music on, barely any other vehicles in sight and I would read or doze whilst she covered the miles. Then we would change over, and I would drive the forest roads while Emma told me to slow down and stop imagining myself to be in a rally car.

And that was how we worked it again on this day.

Emma drove the long route. I fell asleep.

At one point, however, she stopped the car and got out for a minute or two.

I was half-aware of her doing so, but after a quick glance up at the now deep blue sky, I shut my eyes and went back to sleep. Figuring that if we were at the point where we changed seats, Emma would have told me.

Suddenly – it would be unfair to say I heard a scream, because Emma wasn't a screamer – but a cry. Yes. I heard a cry.

I woke immediately and clambered out of the car.

There was Emma. Looking a little pale. And maybe a little short of breath.

"What is it?" I asked, wondering if someone had attacked her in the forest and reaching for my knife. (Carrying knives in Sweden, in the forest, was normal. It could, quite literally, be a matter of life and death.)

"Oh my God", she gasped. "I'm alright. I'm alright".

She leant against the car. Caught her breath. And then, to my surprise. laughed out loud. Only slightly nervously.

"Oh my. Well you were right".

I had no idea what I was right about.

"They are huge aren't they. And somehow, rather cute".

"Who are?" I asked.

"Moose", Emma replied. "Moose. I've just had a very close encounter with one!"

"Where? When? How?"

"Well... Let's just say it's a long way between public conveniences. And this is a very remote spot..."

I nodded. I understood. She didn't need to tell me any more.

"It's quite a shock to find a moose in the loo!" she laughed.

"How close was it?" I asked.

Emma stretched out an arm. "A little bit more than that. But not much".

A few hours later we both saw yet another moose. By now we were driving along the forest roads, looking for an enormous rock which purported to be the entrance to the troll king's lair.

A left turn, a clearing, and there was the rock. We stopped the car to take a look and as we did so, a moose ambled across the car park. We both watched it and laughed. Suddenly they seemed to be everywhere.

As for the rock itself, it must have been all of 20 metres high. One single solid granite boulder.

We had noticed before that the floor of the Swedish forest or *skog* was absolutely littered with boulders of all sizes and shapes. Emma had been reading up about this, and apparently it turned out that the retreating ice of the last ice-age had deposited millions of these things all over what is today Sweden. The forest had then grown up around and through these boulders and now most of them were covered with moss or half-buried by tree-stumps.

It should be noted that these rocks made for an incredibly treacherous walk through the woods. The Swedish *skog* was no

New Forest. This was genuine wilderness. Dangerous even. And frequently impenetrable beyond a few minutes' walk.

This particular boulder was so big and so grand that it was named and there was even a hand-painted wooden sign beside it.

According to the sign, it was a gateway to the underworld. There was a hidden door in the rock which led to the kingdom of trolls and fairies.

We could well believe it.

The emptiness, the stillness, the space, the timelessness and more all flooded in. The air was clean. The forest, to all appearances, was untouched. It was a wilderness, both dangerous and impassable. There were bears and wolves. Lynx and all sorts.

We clambered up onto the top of the rock to admire the view. There was, it has to be said, a wooden staircase going up part of the way. And from the top of that it was a fairly easy scramble to get to the highest point.

In truth the view was a little disappointing. All we could see in every direction was forest. And then more forest. And beyond that in the distance, a glimpse of forest.

But it was nice to see the tops of trees for a change and not just have them towering over us and, as we got to the top, quite suddenly the sun came out once more. The clouds just scattered and there it was. And it was warm. Warm sun. The first time the sun had had any warmth in it so far this year. And what a wonderful sensation it was.

*

The last day of April is, for the Swedes, much what November 5th is for the British. It is Bonfire Night. Only without the fireworks.

Valborgsnatt, or Walpurgis Night to give it its English name, is a festival held in various parts of northern Europe and dates back to a long time before Guy Fawkes night. Festivities vary depending on the country or even the region within a country, but most of them involve burning a large bonfire in public.

Edvard had told us that, long ago, Walpurgis Night was a good excuse for consuming a drink or two. And perhaps taking a girl into the barn for a bit more than a barn dance. Sadly, he had said, these days it was not such a jovial affair.

No doubt some of this was down to the fact that strong alcohol wasn't readily available in Sweden. But on that particular subject there are a few myths that need to be cleared up: before we moved to Sweden we had been told by some of our friends that "you can't buy alcohol over there" and that was that. Some others told us that you could buy it but that it was prohibitively expensive.

Clearly none of them had ever been to Sweden. Because the truth is that lager and other beers are readily available and even more readily consumed. And in fact you can buy reasonably strong alcohol, at prices probably lower than the UK, in any supermarket.

Sadly for Emma and I, both of whom were wine drinkers by choice, wine was not so readily available. And, as with spirits, if you wanted to buy it you had to visit one of the state off-licences – known as Systembolaget.

The Systembolaget is a strange shop. For a start it seems to have no real purpose. Swedes get drunk thanks to the stuff they can buy in supermarkets. And the supermarkets are open all hours, more or less. So we couldn't really understand why it was that the arguably less boozy drinks such as wine were limited to being sold in the state off-licence.

Systembolagets are also pretty rare. In some towns of otherwise decent size, you simply cannot buy wine. They have no Systembolaget. Instead you have to drive maybe an hour or more to the nearest official off-licence in order to get a half bottle of red to go with your pasta. That also seemed odd to us; the strongest drinks were only available to drivers. And you were often required to drive in order to get them.

To further complicate matters, Systembolaget was only open for a few hours here or there on certain days. At other days and hours it was shut. And trying to work out which were which was a game we soon gave up trying to play. Instead, about once every two months we would drive to Copenhagen in neighbouring Denmark and simply fill the car boot up with bottles of wine. Copenhagen was a pleasure to visit anyway, and the cheaper price of the wine made up for petrol costs.

Despite the almost reluctant nature of the state off-licences to part with their stock, given the ready availability of beer, we assumed that special events, such as Walpurgis Night, would still feature at least some alcohol.

Alas, how wrong we were.

Just a few hundred metres from our house was a little football ground. Perhaps calling it a football ground is too grand a term. Really it was just a football pitch. A grassy clearing. There were no stands. On match days, as we would later discover, a hot dog wagon would park near the grass and serve tea, but that was that in terms of facilities.

It was there, on a bit of rough grass next to the football ground, that the Walpurgis Night bonfire was to be lit. Over recent months – going back way before we bought our house – people had been depositing garden waste on the site. And, in recent days, a local farmer had pushed it all together into one huge but vague pile of brushwood and old timber.

It was vast. Certainly the kind of thing which would now have a 200 m perimeter fence back in the UK. It also looked rather fun.

And – being Sweden and not the UK – as there was no perimeter fence, it was also more or less hideously dangerous.

On the last day of April itself, for an hour or so before sunset, which was at about 7 pm, small crowds of people had been drifting past our house on the road from the village. People came in twos or threes. Mostly on foot. Some on bicycles. There were tiny little children and there were gigantic lumberjack types too. There were old women and girls and boys with hair so blond it was almost white.

"I'm looking forward to this", said Emma as we got ourselves ready to go to the fire, "I can see how and why this night meant so much in the old days. After all those weeks of dark and relative isolation, it's kind of bringing people together again".

I was looking forward to it too. I hadn't been to a bonfire party for 20 years or more. And I had many fond memories of them as a child. And even if this one would feature no fireworks, I was looking forward to seeing new faces out and about and enjoying themselves.

"There will be something to eat, won't there?" I asked as I dug out an old coat to wear for standing near the fire, which I knew was going to be a smoky affair.

"Of course", said Emma, "Though probably only hot dogs".

And out we went.

By the time we had walked to the football ground, true to form, we were the last there and the fire had already been lit. The sky was darkening rapidly and we looked around the gathered faces.

The crowd was larger than we had expected. Perhaps two hundred people. And it looked like the cast from that classic Hollywood film 'The Vikings'. Blonde hair and blue eyes in abundance.

We recognised almost no one.

"Do you think all these people live out in the forest through the winter?" whispered Emma, "I've never seen any of them in the shop".

Eventually a bearded man came up to us. He had dark hair. Almost the only person there that did have.

"Hi", he said, "I'm Jack. I live in the village".

We said hello.

"You're the British folk that live in the big house, aren't you?" said Jack.

We said yes and introduced ourselves.

Jack turned out to be a Canadian immigrant. He had moved to Sweden for the love of a Swedish girl way back in the early 1980s. She had long since moved on. Others had come and gone.

But Jack had remained in Sweden and had bought a little house in the village. He was a sculptor by trade.

As we all stood and watched, the big brush-like fire – which had been flickering stubbornly for the last twenty minutes or so and, for all the world, looking more like it was going to go out rather than take hold – suddenly burst into pretty violent life.

Big branches combusted with venom. And small branches turned to flame and disintegrated in seconds.

It was all quite beautiful, really. Dark, low grey clouds. A huge unruly fire, flicking flames a full 30 metres or more into the sky and all those people looking on and – deep inside anyway – celebrating the return of summer.

The crowd, which had been standing round the fire in a circle, much too close really, backed away a little. Not very far, it has to be said. Clearly they were used to these somewhat untamed bonfires.

"Is there somewhere we can buy a drink?" I asked Jack, expecting him to guide us over the nearest beer tent or similar.

He looked at me rather as a doctor might look at a patient to whom he has to give bad news. "A drink? No. Not unless you want to drive to the nearest shop. Which will be closed tonight anyway".

"Food?" asked Emma in a somewhat worried tone.

Jack shook his head. "Nope. Not tonight. Not even hot dogs", he said. And then he added "Look" and pointed at the crowd which, to our total amazement, was already dispersing. Heading home. The fire not yet dying off.

"Goodness me", said Emma, "So much for the days when Walpurgis night was an excuse for drunken debauchery!"

"Edvard and his barns", I added.

"It's kind of ritualistic", said Jack. "Everyone comes. Watches the fire flare up. Then they just leave and go back to their TVs and their houses in the trees".

"I suppose it's something in their blood", I said.

"They do open up a bit more in the summer", said Jack.

We watched as the last few Swedes wandered away, some smiling politely at us. One or two wishing us goodnight.

"I have some American bourbon back at my place", suggested Jack.

We took him up on his offer.

May

Back in the early days of April, Edvard our neighbour had promised us that spring would arrive, on time, during the first week of May. We were unhappy that it hadn't arrived in March and concerned that it had no plans to arrive in April, which is when we normally liked spring to show up, but a promise was a promise and so we waited as patiently as we could.

'As patiently as we could' actually involved increasingly desperate scanning of the sky every morning and getting quite thrilled when one of us saw the smallest flower or if we happened to find a single bud on a tree or plant. "I'm sure that bud wasn't there last week", one of us would say excitedly.

Yes, in fact it was becoming an obsession. And we could see more clearly every day why the Swedish too were obsessed with their weather. It mattered. It wasn't just something that happened. It really mattered!

All the same, it was also getting on my nerves.

"Look", I said one day, angrier with myself than I was with Emma, "One of the reasons we left the UK behind was to get away from the endless talk about the weather and the rain. And yet here we are, pretty much every day now, checking the blasted thermometers and searching the skies for glimpses of sun".

Emma agreed. "True. But at least it doesn't rain here".

And that was true. That was something positive.

It seemed somehow strange. Sweden was further north than most of the UK. And it was a lot greyer and colder – at least it was in the winter. Logically, so it seemed to us, it ought to rain a lot more too. But it didn't. It was much, much drier than the UK.

In fact this turned out to be due to Norway standing in the way of the rain as it came across the North Sea from Britain. Sweden is in a rain shadow. Most of it is anyway. And that particular discovery, once again courtesy of the internet, gave us a few hours of feeling smug.

However, regardless of finding such crumbs of comfort, the joy soon wore off and we persisted with our search for spring.

Each day would bring yet more "Oohs" and "Aahs" over the sight of a bird possibly building a nest, a feeling of some warmth in the sunshine or the sound of a bee buzzing by. Or was it a bee? It might just be a bluebottle. We were no longer sure. We just wanted spring to arrive. The Swedish winter needed to go and to go now. We were slowly going under.

And then, of course, true to Swedish efficiency (which is, arguably, every bit as good as the famous German efficiency), on one day – the 7th of May, to be exact – there it was. Spring had arrived.

The sun came out and it had real warmth in it. But that wasn't all. We found flowers. Real flowers. And the grass was turning green again after very many months of being a dull sort of brownish yellow.

And by the end of that single, long warm day, buds had appeared and turned green. And yes, this time, for sure, a bee had buzzed and got itself stuck inside the house. (We didn't mind. We were so pleased to see it that we almost put out a cup of tea or a glass of aquavit for the little insect to drink.)

All that, suddenly, in just one day.

And over the course of the next few days the whole landscape changed.

So far we had only seen Sweden laden with snow. Beautiful but stark. And that had been followed by Sweden without snow. Bare and dark. Rather dreary to be honest.

But in the space of a week in early May all that changed.

Suddenly every tree was covered with bright green leaves. There were flowers popping up in every garden. The forest lost its ragged look and became an ever-denser wall of green.

Of course the spruce and pine had been green all winter. But they were a harsh dark green. A mass of gloom really inhabited solely – or so it seemed – by hordes of biting flies. But now much of that gloom was lost behind a curtain of fine green as trees like willow, hazel, beech and birch sprung back into life. We didn't really know what the different trees or flowers were. We didn't care either. We were just so pleased to see them.

Then a squirrel. A real one. A red one. The first we had ever seen. It came chirruping and chattering down the tree closest to our house, presumably awoken by the noise, sights, smells and warmth of the arrival of spring.

We both sat and watched it as it ran back and forth collecting things. Or so we assumed. It was a joy to see.

The only problem was that the squirrel seemed to have woken from its hibernation in a foul temper. On a short flagpole near the steps outside the front door, we had a smallish Swedish flag. Most Swedish houses have full sized flags and flagpoles. The deep blue and yellow of their national flag looks quite wonderful against the pale blue skies of winter. We wanted one too but, as yet, had gotten no further than buying this token flagstaff.

We liked our little flag. But the squirrel clearly wasn't equally impressed. And every time he ran past the thing, to gather nuts or whatever, he stopped to jump up and grab hold of the it and tug at it quite viciously. In fact, on about the third pass, he took such a robust hold of the flag that he tore a big piece of it off.

"What's he doing?!" laughed Emma, as we watched from our window. We couldn't be angry with the little fellow, it was too comical for that.

"He must be tearing it up to make bedding out of it", I suggested.

But no. Each time he tore a piece of the flag off, he dropped down and ran off, leaving the torn fragments to just blow away.

"He must have been hibernating within earshot of it", I laughed, "And the endless flapping and snapping of the flag all winter must have annoyed him, only he was too warm or sleepy to get up out of his bed to do anything about it".

"That must be it!" replied Emma through tears of laughter, "Or maybe he's a German squirrel and doesn't like the Swedish flag. Edvard said that there were quite a few Germans living in the area!"

A few days after the squirrel had destroyed our flag, the first lawnmowers of spring also made their appearance.

Even in rugged Sweden, thick with forest and littered with rocks to climb and lakes to swim, many men still have very little outlet for their masculinity in the modern world and the sit-on lawnmower seems to somehow fulfil that function for some of these men.

With the coming of spring and the appearance of greenery, such men are finally able to leave behind the central heating, flowery patterned wallpaper, dado rails and immense TV screens and are once again able to get 'out there' into the wild and do things with nature. Although admittedly that mostly involves destroying it.

Of course it was still too early in the year for petrol driven strimmers and the ubiquitous BBQ; such things were still in the garage gathering dust and would remain there until June. But those first few bright shoots of grass had obviously rattled a few cages or dug at some deep-seated desire to show prowess and so, that very weekend, with lawns having barely felt the sun on their green backs, the mowers were out in force to cut them down again.

It wasn't that we minded, particularly. After all we only had one close neighbour and Edvard didn't show the same passion for cutting grass that others did. He only had a small patch of grass and seemed to be much keener on shrubs and flowers than his lawn. But there was something strangely disquieting about the sudden release of all these machines throughout the village itself.

Fifty houses or so. Each, seemingly, with a little mower. Each mowing – as we soon discovered – two or even three times a week. All those little petrol engines. Noise. Fumes. And for what? Just to keep an overly large patch of grass right down at crew-cut level. Somehow it didn't seem to fit with the much-publicised Swedish concern for the environment and nature.

All the same it brought my attention to my own garden – field to be more precise – and I wondered if there was anything I could or should do to make my own piece of the world somehow more 'me'.

I had begun my vegetable patch back in April, and I had sown the first seeds. All of that had taken place much later than it would have done in more temperate climes but I had researched it a little and all was as it should be.

But out beyond my growing clearing of vegetable beds there was still an awful lot of wild and unruly grass that was, like it or not, my responsibility.

"I'm going to plant some fruit trees", I said, "And let a lot of the grass grow wild too. So that birds and bees and things can have somewhere to live".

It was a good idea. All around was forest. And what wasn't forest was now very, very well behaved lawns. So anything that liked to live in long grass really had nowhere to go. Which was strange, given the size and emptiness of the country.

Emma agreed with me. We would have a wildflower meadow. "But what else are you going to do?" she asked. "Leaving some of the grass to grow is a nice thought. But it can do that without your help. The garden, the land, probably needs a bit more work than that."

It was true. She was right.

It would take just half an hour to demarcate an area to leave to grow wild. I could cut the rest – about 5,000m2 – with a lawnmower. And we already had one of those. It had been left behind by the previous owners. But trees, flowers, shrubs, structure, all of the things that gave shape and form to a garden at needed to be put in. It wouldn't appear by itself.

"Why don't you start by putting a gate at the end of the drive?" Emma suggested. "It would help stop the car headlights shining into the house in the evenings".

About twenty cars a day went past our house. So that wasn't really much of an issue. But I could see what she meant and I saw no reason not to put in a gate.

And what a fateful moment that was.

"Let's go and look for a nice gate in a DIY shop this afternoon", I said, "And we can have a cup of tea somewhere too".

Sweden is a modern country. Yet in many ways it's very similar to the UK of the 1960s and 1970s. For example, during the daytime there are no men or women of working age to be seen. They all have jobs. Either that or they all hide indoors. So that wherever you go, during the daytime, only old folk and the odd mother with a baby can be seen.

It's a nice feeling. It feels somehow right that people of working age are... well... *at work* and working. Obviously things may be a little different to that in the three big cities, but out in the vast majority of the country, that certainly seems to hold true.

Similarly, Sweden seems to be a remarkably safe and trusting country too – again in much the same way the UK once was. Keys are readily loaned to neighbours, houses in the forest are often left unlocked, deckchairs, boats and fishing equipment are all left by lakes and along the seashore, crime rates are low, traffic levels are low. And so on. And so on. All in all the country seems to have a very positive and very encouraging outlook on life.

Unfortunately, in many ways the shops in Sweden also resemble the UK in the 1960s and 1970s. Or perhaps even the 1950s. They all have a very limited stock of products and, no matter how far you travel, they all seem to sell exactly the same few things.

One example of this was the door handle.

Our front door was old. And the handle was damaged. So we wanted to replace it.

Without making a specific trip to find a replacement, we looked in about a dozen different shops to find a nice new handle.

And every single shop that did sell door handles sold exactly the same rather ugly model in exactly the same faux-brass colour.

In the end we asked whether any others could be ordered. We received a very puzzled response. Why would we want any other type? But, yes, if we really did want something different, the same handle could also be bought in black. Did we want that?

In the end we just bought a faux-brass one. What did it really matter? It was only a door handle.

As time went by, however, we realised that this lack of choice applied to a lot more than just door handles. We couldn't buy a length of copper pipe for beneath the sink because we weren't registered plumbers. We couldn't get roller blinds in any colour other than dark blue or white – and our room was suited to neither colour. We liked variety in food but wherever we went to a supermarket the only butter available was from the Central Dairy – it came in two types; salted or partially salted. The same with ham. It was smoked. Or you didn't have ham. The same with fish. Smoked. Or no fish. There were few organic options, no locally produced options, no variety even of labels.

Foolishly, with the gate, I had subconsciously decided to make a stand against this Sovietesque monopoly: I wanted a nice gate for my drive. Something wooden. It didn't have to be all that special, just nice. Solid. Handsome. Perhaps a little bit different from the norm.

And so, later that day, we visited the two local DIY shops. There were only two. But neither of them had any gates. Nor did the local garden centres which Emma and I visited a few days later. Nor did the local timber yard, which I made a point of visiting the following week. No one had a gate. And Edvard had no idea where we might buy one. In fact he was surprised to hear us talk about both gates and buying gates in almost equal measure when I spoke to him about it, having just come back from the timer yard.

"Why do you need a gate?" he asked us. "Surely no one is troubling you? And the animals will come onto your garden of course even if you have one".

I assured Edvard that no one was giving us any trouble, I told him I was more than happy for moose to cross my land (as they all now regularly did) and I tried to explain about the car headlights – but that explanation seemed weak even to me. The truth was that, by now, I had gotten a 'bee in my bonnet' about buying the damned thing and nothing was going to stop me.

"I think most people would maybe make themselves one", said Edvard, "If they really needed one. I made my own". We looked at it. It looked homemade. He was happy with it. But I wanted something a bit less flimsy, a bit more statement-y.

"Let's just not bother", said Emma after I came back from Edvard's and told her about his suggestion. "There aren't that many cars. We don't really need a gate".

Clearly she had a better appreciation or, at least, a more honest appreciation of what my own hand-made gate might look like. Despite my practical skills, which were not inconsiderable, woodworking was probably at the bottom of my list.

"No", I said, "I want a gate. And I'm going to get one. One way or another".

The saga of the gate had begun. Little did I realise how long a saga it would be.

*

One Saturday afternoon in late May, Emma needed to post a few parcels. We had already been out that morning to do our shopping for the weekend, and neither of us felt like driving again. So that meant a quick visit to the village shop – which also served as a post office. It was a pleasant afternoon, the sun was shining, and I knew that Carina would be working in the shop, so I decided to walk up to the village with Emma.

The walk was always pleasant anyway, along the leafy bridle path, and just a good sort of distance to make you feel that you had had some exercise.

The shop was on the ground floor of a large – and fairly ugly – wooden building painted Falun red. Above it was a small flat, and underneath it, in the cellar, was an even smaller 'clubhouse'. The latter was a members only venue. At least, that was the legal status of the place. And being members only meant it was allowed to play live music at weekends and serve alcohol. In practice anyone who lived in the village was an honorary member, as was anyone who visited at the weekend to watch a band. For some reason or another, we had yet to visit the little 'clubhouse' but now that it was almost summer, and there were some interesting looking bands coming up, we promised ourselves that we would get around to it.

Outside the shop, on most Saturday mornings, in the car park, you could buy hot dogs prepared over an extremely black barbecue by a rotating team of villagers. It was a shame that they always did hot dogs, as they were – at best – a pretty depressing sort of food, but at least these were freshly grilled, with the sausages from a local producer and were consequently a cut above the norm.

Local events, ranging from tea dances, to blood donations, were advertised on a board outside the shop too. And petrol was sold from the forecourt – which, for a small village shop, in the middle of nowhere, was quite an important service. (Small things like that, which in a more crowded country, with towns and services all over the place might be taken for granted, could, quite literally, mean the difference between life and death in a big empty land like Sweden).

Once inside, to my mind, the shop was exactly what I would have expected the interior of a shop in Alaska to look like. It was dark. Cluttered. Clad from top to bottom in pine. And it sold everything from clothes pegs to boot polish and tinned pineapple to *sill* (in jars, in assorted overly sugary flavours).

A local baker had recently started making very good sourdough loaves, and we frequently bought one of these rather than the mass produced stuff usually available in the supermarkets. (Although, to be fair, even those supermarkets often sold similar heavy bread, freshly made, when they could get it.) Today, however, the bread was already all sold out, which was a bit disappointing.

In fact, as Emma and I looked around the store, we realised that quite a few of the more perishable products were sold out. That was unusual. And with just a tin or two in our hands, and Emma's parcels to post, we asked Carina if there was a problem with supplies.

"No", Carina answered, as she rang up the till for the few things we were buying, "No. It is more that we will close early today. And not open tomorrow, Sunday, as usual. So people have been in to buy things and also for their parties".

"Oh, parties? Why's that then?" Emma asked, as she went behind the counter to do the calculations for the postage. "It's not a national holiday, is it?"

Carina came out from behind the counter. Her huge pile of blonde hair was folded up on top of her head, making her piercingly blue eyes – and suntan – appear even more startling than usual.

"No", said Carina, clearly very excited about the prospect, "It is for the Eurovision of course. It's tonight!"

Although we don't really watch TV, neither Swedish nor British, back in March we had noticed a lot of talk about something called 'Melodifestivalen' which we had assumed was a local Swedish song contest. This, it had turned out, was actually the qualifying tournament for Eurovision. And, in Sweden, it was huge. Songs were written in summer, entries submitted, whittled down to a short list of about 20 or so. And then, over a few weeks in late winter or early spring, these were televised and the 'best' of them selected to go forward as Sweden's entry for Eurovision.

They took the thing pretty seriously. Some might even say they took it too seriously.

Emma and I knew a little about this, but we had yet to talk to a Swede about it. And now seemed as good a chance as any.

"Shall I pour us all a coffee?" I asked.

The corner of the shop was given over to a small seating area where coffee and biscuits were available at a very nominal price.

Carina sat down and I poured all three of us a coffee. Emma came over – having sorted out the postage – and I passed the biscuit jar around.

"Is it a very big event then? Eurovision?" I asked.

"Oh yes", Carina replied, "All over Europe".

"No", said Emma, "I think he means, is it a very important event here, in Sweden. For the Swedish".

Carina nodded. "Oh, yes. I think so. Almost a national holiday, as you say. But not quite. But as it is always at the weekend, we treat it like a national day. All people will be getting together with their families and friends to watch it tonight."

My biscuit chose that moment to snap in half and flop into my coffee with a small splash.

Carina saw it and laughed. "Two years ago, Sweden won. And there were lots of parties in the street afterwards. In the towns. People drinking champagne and jumping into the fountain".

To Emma and I, coming from 'nil points' England, it seemed almost unbelievable. In the UK, whilst a fair number of people enjoyed the show itself, I don't think anyone, ever, would drink champagne and dance in a fountain if a modern day Bucks Fizz took first prize in Eurovision. We would probably all go to bed an hour later having completely forgotten about it.

"Sometimes", Carina continued, "We open the club, underneath this shop, to watch the show. It can be a lot of fun".

Sadly, this year, the club was not going to be hosting the event, as there was an ongoing problem of some sort with a water leak. But in future, for sure, Emma and I would watch Eurovision along with the rest of the village in the cellar underneath the shop.

Later that evening, sitting down to watch Eurovision via the internet with the usual disdainful British commentary, I did a little research into Sweden and the song contest. And, to my surprise, it seemed that Carina was quite right. Some Swedes took defeat very seriously, more or less in the same manner that the English took an international football defeat (usually on penalties) very seriously. It would be talked about for days or even weeks afterwards in the news. Similarly, success was also taken very seriously. In the UK, if you won Eurovision (not that anyone did any more), you still risked being wholly forgotten by the following Tuesday. But in Sweden, if you sung and you won, you were made for life. As long as you were happy to sing your winning tune for the rest of your days, you could easily build a financially very successful career. In music or otherwise. People would buy albums or read your books. If you became a hairstylist, your products would be guaranteed to succeed. It was as if, by winning Eurovision, you had somehow been touched by the gods. The old Norse gods, presumably.

Oddly, just as the Swedish entry was about to start singing, I also spotted something else on the internet. Doing a very quick Google search on Carina, I found that our village shop was being staffed not only by someone who was incredibly efficient, polite and popular, but that she had once sung an entry for the Swedish melody festival – and finished a creditable third place. Not only that but she was also a bit part actress on TV. And had recently had several non-speaking roles in the Swedish version of the Wallender police series. Sweden, clearly, was a land of opportunity.

*

The last few days of May were very sunny and quite warm. It was still cooler than late May usually was in the UK, but the clearness of the sky and the freshness of the air made up for it, and the dryness of the air made the temperatures feel warmer than they actually were.

For me, however, those last few days of May weren't about the weather. They were about the gate. I decided to make a further attempt at getting one.

We had heard good reports from both Edvard and Carina about a big reclamation yard not far from where we lived. Apparently, it sold just about everything imaginable, from a big red barn.

I should digress here and first say something about Swedish barns. Barns may be big in the UK. They may be big in other countries too, for all I know, but in Sweden they're frequently the size of aircraft hangars! The reason for this is that sometimes quite large herds of cows, have to be kept indoors from about the start of October until about the start of April due to the harsh climate. And, obviously, all those animals spending a whole long winter indoors, in one space, require a little bit of elbowroom. Not to mention room for food and toilets. Hence many barns in Sweden are truly vast.

Stellet, the reclamation yard, was one such barn. In fact it was three such barns. And as we approached it, we immediately knew that we had found the right place. Because outside, hidden amongst a collection of old cars, caravans, pushbikes and mile after mile of rusting iron 'stuff', there was a full-sized, concrete municipal staircase. The kind of thing that would have once led to a busy 1960s town hall or law courts. And painted on the side of the staircase in great big black letters was 'Ej till salu'; not for sale.

"Why do you think they want to keep that, and not sell it?" asked Emma as we got out of the car.

I couldn't imagine. "Perhaps they have a client in Poland or Russia or somewhere like that who's been looking for something just like it and now they're just waiting for him to arrange transport". It did have an Eastern bloc sort of feel to it.

In fact the truth was probably quite different to that. Because once we got inside, squeezing past old sofas, tables and other assorted fire-risks piled high, we noticed that quite a few things – usually the more hideous of them – had 'ej till salu' written on them too.

"The owner must be a jackdaw", whispered Emma.

Once inside the place it also became apparent that what Carina and Edvard had told us was true; everything in the world was on show here. Everything. All at once. And most of it had been there since before time began.

It would be as futile to try and describe what was in those three barns as it would be to try and list everything that there is in the world at this point in time. Those three huge barns have the lot, probably including things that don't actually exist anywhere else in the world, and never have done.

Suffice to say that the owner was clearly pretty keen on keeping most of his stock where it was. Lots of it was marked as not for sale, but much more was marked up as if the owner had thought of a figure and multiplied it by a few thousand. Obviously this was a place where bartering was the only way to get a good deal.

My search through the world of relics took me past quite a few items that probably belonged in a museum. Were the missing Faberge eggs in here? Was that a real Gauguin or just a good copy? Had I needed to equip an infantry division, here were the uniforms and even the bayonets. But I managed to somehow brave all that, pick almost none of it up, and press on past old doors and windows (the doors still with those same handles, despite being ancient) and out into the rearmost yard where great concrete and stone things stood and probably had stood since the last ice age.

It was out here, amongst fencing, old railway sleepers and one of the world's largest collections of prams that I would find myself 'the gate'.

No, in fact it wasn't.

Nothing was a gate.

Box after box of tiles, piles of wood, old farming equipment, cages for keeping birds in, a big cage that could have once contained a lion, mounds of gravel, piles of bricks, benches, chairs, umbrellas dating back to the 1800s, pipes – all sorts of pipes – fastenings made of iron, even a pile of what looked like German WWII jackboots.

But no gate.

I suppose, had we stopped at that point, we could just have put it all down to experience. But no. Emma had seen a chaise longue type of thing that did, admittedly, have a certain charm. And she wanted it.

The owner wouldn't move on the price – which would have kept him in hot dogs for quite some time to come. But Emma bought it anyway.

A day or two later it arrived at our home.

A day or two after that we lit our first bonfire and burned the damned thing. It had more animal life in it than London Zoo – most of which either jumped or drilled small holes in wood.

I wasn't about to give up on the gate, however. And as the end of the month arrived, I found a gate, online, that was – ostensibly – available in Sweden, from a German company, and could even be delivered.

I placed my order and switched the computer off. And May finished with my feeling just a little bit pleased with myself. I had done it. All it had taken was a little perseverance. Or so I thought.

June

Our first visitors arrived in June.

Somehow we had imagined that, by living abroad, we would be
swamped with long lost relatives, friends and acquaintances. But
that hadn't happened. We had seen no one. And as the dark cold
grey days of winter had turned into the largely cold dark grey
days of spring, we had begun to think that it was something
personal.

But of course it wasn't that. It was something to do with Sweden
itself. In fact there were probably several factors at work.

On the one hand Sweden just isn't on the radar for most people.
France is just across the water from the UK. Spain is somewhere
everyone has visited. Italy and Greece offer all kinds of treasures
in terms of food and sights. But what do most people know about
Sweden? Ask any man and he will mention Swedish women. Ask
any woman and she will probably mention Abba.

And then there is the mistaken belief that Sweden is an expensive
country. It isn't. Not really. Some things are expensive. Some
things aren't. Norway is expensive. Sweden isn't.

And even if some of that is a bit of a generalisation, it remains true that for most people, if they have a spare week or weekend in February or April, and the money to travel, they are likely to visit somewhere warm and sunny rather than catch a plane to somewhere potentially darker and greyer than Britain.

However, while it may be true that Swedish winters are long and very cold, with lots of snow, and springs are almost non-existent, just a brief hiccough between the end of winter and the start of summer, those summers, Swedish summers, are just as hot as they are in the UK – and often very much sunnier and a lot drier too. And, in those summers, Sweden has another advantage too; the sun is up for something like 18 hours a day.

We had told Tom and Judy all this before they visited.

So when they arrived on the first weekend of June and found it cold, wet and grey they were disappointed. They had expected sun and summer. And lots of it.

I had known Tom since my schooldays. Like me, he had worked in a factory after leaving school and, again like me, he had then decided to return to university in order to find a better career. He'd had more success than I had and he was now a clinical psychologist and had even had some books published. But this was the first time he had taken a holiday so far north.

"I can't believe how much forest there is", were pretty much the first words he said. "I've never seen anything like it. All the way from the airport, on the train, to here, all we could see was forest. It's amazing!"

"We can't wait to get out into it and have a long walk" added Judy enthusiastically, "Only last week we went for a long walk in Dovedale in Derbyshire. It's so rugged and so pretty there".

Outside, the rain was falling in thick grey sheets. And behind the livelier green of willows and beech, the dark green walls of the forest looked almost black and very impenetrable. Rugged, certainly. Pretty it was not. Not today, least ways.

"The thing is", said Emma, "It's not really like Dovedale here. This lot, the forest, goes all the way from here more or less unbroken to the Arctic Circle. That's about 1000 miles of unbroken dark woodland..."

Judy wasn't to be put off. "We'll go for a walk just as soon as this rain eases off".

Three days passed. We mainly spent them talking about the old days and eating and drinking, and the rain didn't ease up for a moment. On the fourth day I came downstairs to find Judy in her waterproof trousers and jacket and Tom just about to pull on his walking boots.

"Are you coming with us?" asked Judy.

I didn't want to, but I knew that I would have to. Neither of them had any idea what the forest, this sort of forest – *skog* – was really like. I was hardly an expert myself, but I knew that in most directions it was impossible to walk for more than a hundred metres before you had to turn back.

There were hazards, too. In one direction there was a genuine bog partially hidden under the trees. A wrong step there and it was mud up to the waist if not beyond. It was also the kind of walk where you could break an ankle at any time, thanks to the crazy paving left behind by the last Ice Age. And so it made sense to walk in threes, if at all possible, just in case something like that happened and one person had to stay behind with the injured one while the third went for help.

Then there were the mosquitoes. And gnats, adders and other assorted nasties. Some of these you just had to take your chance with. Make a loud enough noise and the adders would disappear long before you trod on them. But the biting flies? That was another story. I had already learned that the rain drove them into a kind of frenzy. They bit for fun when it was like this. And the only thing to do was stay indoors.

Failing that, if you really had to go out there, especially when it was raining, it was essential to cover up and dose any uncovered skin in something called Mygga.

And that was what I did.

Mygga was a sort of roll-on anti-perspirant for flies. Or, rather, not for flies. It smelt a little strange at first, but after a few months in Sweden and several walks in the *skog*, I had gotten used to it.

Judy, however, was adamant that the flies would not bite that much and that, even if they did, the Mygga stuff wouldn't keep them off.

I insisted she put the stuff on anyway. But she was even more insistent that she wouldn't do so.

And so it was that we all set out in the rain and into the darkest woods in Europe.

I led the way, as I knew of a track that took us past the swampy section and up onto a clearing above a lake. It was a nice walk, gentle and with a good view at the end of it, which really could show anyone just what Sweden was all about.

A little way into the walk, I knew that flies were with us. They whizz and ping close by and, by doing so, give themselves away. So I dug into my little backpack and brought out a couple of pairs of gloves. We were all walking with sticks, which seemed de rigueur, and so I was wearing gloves to protect my exposed hands and I suggested that Tom and Judy wear them too. I knew from my own experience that a mosquito bite on the hand could be very uncomfortable indeed.

Tom, who had already been pestered by a few small flies, took my advice.

Judy, who knew the countryside better than anyone else – or so she liked to think – still refused my help.

The walk to the top of the small hill – Cardiac Ridge, as Emma and I called it; the same hill I had failed to ski down – was pleasant, despite the rain.

We stopped a few times and looked at troll-like figures in the woods. We heard something barking – which we all hoped was a deer. And we found the most enormous ants, living in the biggest anthill, that any of us had ever seen. These ants were big enough to put a saddle on. Any bigger and they could have had a jockey as well!

At the top of the ridge, we sat and ate a few sandwiches and looked at the view. Tom and I laughed about how we had once done the same, in the centre of Birmingham, sitting in a small but noisy park surrounded by cars and the usual city bedlam. By contrast here there was nothing. For better and worse. No traffic, no crime, no pubs to sit in, no food nearby, no comforts, no noise, no internet, no armchairs, no music, nothing but fresh air, wildlife, trees and space. And flies.

The walk up to the ridge and back wasn't all that far and it didn't too take long. Maybe three hours in total, because we also wandered down to the lake and spent a little time there.

But already, by the time we got back to the house, three or four bites were coming up quite badly on Judy's face and hands.

There was nothing we could now do for her. Creams and antiseptics didn't really help. In fact there were no creams. Not in Sweden. If you got bitten, you had to put up with the most furious itching and even, sometimes, swelling that you could imagine.

There was, in truth, only one way to be sure of getting a good night's sleep once you had such bites. And that evening, over a game or two of Monopoly we all made sure that Judy drank more than her fair share of Aquavit. So much so that by the time the rest of us all went to bed, she was already fast asleep on the sofa and covered over with a couple of blankets.

It would still itch like hell over the next few days, but at least she would get one good night's sleep.

*

Despite the bites and despite the rain – which, very unusually for Sweden persisted throughout most of that early June fortnight – Judy enjoyed her stay immensely. In fact the country itself won both her and Tom over. Its sheer size, wildness and freshness was something they both promised to come and see again. And on the last night of their holiday, they insisted on taking us all out for a meal at a restaurant.

"Where do you recommend?" asked Judy, "We'll treat you to dinner at your favourite place".

The truth was we didn't have a favourite place. In France, yes. Greece too. In Italy we had always enjoyed eating out. But our one visit to the restaurant in Kalmar had dampened any enthusiasm to explore the culinary delights of Sweden very much further.

Nevertheless Tom and Judy easily persuaded us that we should try somewhere else, and they assured us that everywhere had bad restaurants and that the one in Kalmar was obviously just one of those.

Of course they were right. So we spent a half hour on the internet looking for somewhere to eat in Växjö, the nearest large town.

On the drive to the place – which will remain unnamed – Emma and I warned Tom and Judy that drinks in the restaurant, wine to be specific, would be very expensive. We also talked for a while about the drink driving laws in Sweden, and in Scandinavia in general. The laws were pretty strict. In Norway, so we had heard, there were even waiting lists for people to go to prison for a few weeks because – for a first offence of drink driving in Norway – by all accounts you do a short stint in a cell.

It wouldn't matter tonight, however, because I was driving and I wouldn't drink and drive.

The restaurant itself was, ostensibly anyway, somewhere that did "Traditional Swedish food" as well as a few of the more usual and contemporary offerings featuring the ubiquitous pasta.

A long time ago, back in my early student days, I had studied Sweden a little bit and learned a little of the language and culture. Back then, reading some Strindberg plays, I had come across various traditional Swedish dishes which had appealed to me. *Sjömans Biff* was one and *Kalops* was another.

Sjömans Biff (literally Sailor's Beef and pronounced 'Phew-Mans-Beef') is one of Sweden's most well-known dishes. Originally cooked in one pot in the galley on a ship, it's a fairly simple stew which, when done well, ought to be really tasty. With beef and beer and not much else other than good potatoes and onions, there really isn't a lot that can go wrong with it.

Kalops (pronounced as it looks) is another stew. Also a great old classic which should be cooked slowly. It's also another beef dish, though sometimes it can be made with meat such as venison. The key ingredient for kalops – apart from having good ingredients, which all food needs – is allspice.

Of course it was June, and stew wouldn't normally have been our first choice for a meal out. But this June had been cold and grey so far and the opportunity to finally eat some of these foods I had once read about was too good to miss.

The restaurant itself seemed quite nice. Dark, but not so dark that they were trying to hide the food. Warm but fresh too. And there was, thankfully, a definite smell of cooking coming from the kitchens, something that had been sadly lacking from the restaurant in Kalmar.

Unfortunately, as things turned out, it might have been better if there hadn't been a smell of cooking. Because whoever was doing it didn't know how to cook. Or what to cook. Or why. When. At what temperature or, so it seemed, anything else.

The wine, to be fair, wasn't too expensive and it was pretty good. A Gaillac from the south west of France and one of my favourites. Because I was driving, I had to sit and watch as the others enjoyed it – but that's what friends sometimes have to do.

And then the food arrived. And things went downhill from there.

I had Sailor's Beef. But it didn't seem to contain beef. And I think any self-respecting sailor would have chucked the cook overboard. This wasn't slow cooked in one pot. This was fried. Fried meat, probably pork, and, not surprisingly given that they were fried, undercooked potatoes. I also wondered what the great pool of mayonnaise was doing on the island of meat. Would a ship have added that back in the days of blisters, tall masts and sails?

Emma's kalops wasn't much better. In fact, after tasting both, I came to the conclusion that the kalops was the sailor's beef but without the mayonnaise. It certainly didn't contain any allspice. It had ginger. It had cumin. And even a little chilli. But allspice hadn't yet entered the building. Or, at least, if it was in the building it hadn't yet found its way to the kitchen.

Emma and I toyed with the food for a while, but we were relieved when the waiter came and took the still largely full plates away.

Neither Tom nor Judy had chosen the traditional Swedish foods and so they had escaped the dubious delights that Emma and I had just been presented with. (It would be inaccurate to say 'just eaten'.) However their food – with pasta – didn't seem to be that much better, either in terms of being edible or well-cooked or well presented.

Dessert, again, as in Kalmar, was largely sugar, served with something that seemed to be a smoked wafer. What it was supposed to be, none of us had any idea. And so, at the end of the night, the only thing any of us had had that we enjoyed at all was the wine. Which, as the driver, I had totally missed out on. I decided that the next time we ate in a Swedish restaurant – if there ever was a next time – it would be Emma's turn to drive.

*

As our first visitors left, so the summer proper arrived. It was now mid-June and, once again right on cue, the Swedish weather did what it was expected to do. The rain stopped on the very day that our friends flew back to the UK and the Swedish schools broke up for their long two month summer holiday.

We wondered if having a well-behaved and predictable climate helps to shape a well-behaved and predictable people? That could explain a lot about different countries.

To us, the school holidays seemed to be quite long in Sweden. We weren't certain about this as we neither had children nor worked at a Swedish job with Swedish holidays. But we had formed the distinct impression that the Swedes got used, at an early age, to taking a lot of time off. There was, for example, the two months in summer. The same period which more or less defined summer proper in Sweden. During this period – which finished in mid-August – hotel prices went up, ice cream kiosks opened, boat trips (such as there were) extended their opening hours and the campsites got busy.

Adults weren't quite as fortunate as Swedish children. But even so, they were still entitled to a three-week break in the summer. Which seemed eminently sensible to us as, being the nicest time of year, it made sense to concentrate holidays during that period.

But they also seemed to have had quite a while off around February. During that month various people from around the village had disappeared for a while, pretty clearly to somewhere hot and sunny. And one by one the likes of Olof, Carina, Johan and others all re-appeared in that gloomy time of the year with a fine sun tan.

Another difference we had noticed in Swedish employment culture seemed to be starting times and, of course, finishing times. Rush hour was from six o'clock to about seven thirty am. And by 8 am everyone seemed to be at work. Likewise by 4 pm, offices and so forth were closed for the day and everyone was on their way back home again.

Emma and I had wondered whether this was to do with avoiding driving in the dark or something like that. But it was dark at those times of day anyway, for six months of the year, so we figured it must be for some other reason that the Swedish got up and went out to work so early and came back so soon.

There certainly were differences between their outlook on the world and that which we had grown up with. Employment was more unionised in Sweden, and meetings took place to discuss things between managers and staff on a regular basis. In fact, from what we had heard, many Swedes thought that there were far too many of these meetings and that, if they met a bit less often, they might get a bit more work done.

Something else that struck us, both in winter but ever more so as the year warmed up, was the obvious passion the Swedish had for being outdoors.

True, for many men, this did take the form of mowing the lawn at every available opportunity. And, once summer really showed its hand, on days where the mowers were at rest, the strimmers hacked and maimed any other kind of undergrowth in the garden.

And yes, there were also BBQs a-plenty. Once again, these were apparent from the first nice day onwards but really came into their own during the hot summer months.

But there was more to it than that.

It seemed to us that, at pretty much every available opportunity, the Swedish would also dig out old cars (often old American cars of which there were very many) or motorbikes and – with empty roads in front of them – take these things out for a spin just for fun.

The same was also true of boats. More houses had boats than I cared to count. Big ones, little ones. All sorts of boats. Often these were left down by a lake or even down on the beach by the sea. But, as with the old cars and motorbikes, they were regularly used when the sun came out and the temperature went up.

Then there were the *sommarstugor,* a wholly new concept to us. A *sommarstuga* (literally a summer cottage) is a place where the Swedish live during the summer. These can vary from things not much larger than a garden shed to full blown palaces. Invariably they are in the forest or by the sea. And, often, they are left uninhabited throughout the rest of the year.

Very many Swedish own one of these summer cottages. And most spend at least a few weeks there in the summer. But what really surprised us about them was that quite a good number of these buildings seemed to be lived in throughout the whole of the summer. Such that Swedes who normally lived in flats in the towns (which most did) moved out to their summer cottages for a few months and commuted to work from these places instead. It was all a part of the outdoor culture which so many Swedes seemed to enjoy.

After living for about six months in the country we could see how both flats and cottage fitted into the Swedish psyche. Sweden was a land of order and a land of freedom. It was both. It was all about structure and all about fresh air. Being Swedish meant keeping clean but also getting dirty in an ordered sort of way.

Such was also the case with that most traditional of Swedish festivals; Midsommar. The biggest outdoor event of the Swedish calendar.

Traditionally Midsommar has always been a big celebration in Sweden, and all sorts of stuff can be read about it on the internet. As with most old traditions, it was once a good excuse for a few hours away from work and an excess of alcohol and, if lucky, a visit to one of the vast barns with the best looking girl (or guy) from the village. But these days it was (sadly) a much more sober affair. Something for families and tourists rather than lusty young farmers and serving wenches.

Despite it being the single largest outdoor public event in the country, a must-do for everyone, something not to be missed, our first Swedish Midsommar was a no-show because Emma had to go back to the UK and clear up a few business related issues. And by the time she would be back, the maypoles and fiddles would all be hidden away again for another 12 months.

All the same, and despite being alone on the night itself, I was determined to enjoy my midsummer somehow.

Midsummer's day is, of course, the longest day of the year. A time to celebrate summer and the sun. And even in southern Sweden – assuming it isn't a washout – that means there is enough light to sit in your garden at midnight and read a book. And a few nights before midsummer that's exactly what I decided to do. In a local bookshop I had found an old copy of a Strindberg play – Miss Julie – and decided to sit out all night long in a hammock and read it from cover to cover.

So as the sun set on the longest day of the year and things grew stiller than usual, a glass or two of aquavit and Miss Julie made for ideal companions.

Ironically the play itself is set at midsummer, back in the days when the celebration was still on the 'lively' side. And as I sat and read it, up to and past midnight, wrapped in a thin blanket, and as the aquavit slowly worked its potent spells on my mind, I wondered how much of modern Sweden August Strindberg would recognise.

The night was mild. Warm even. There were some strange soft sounds from the *skog* – of animals doing whatever they did at midsummer – but other than that nothing. It was heavenly.

I had another glass of aquavit and fell asleep for an hour or two in my hammock.

Suddenly at about 3.00 am, I awoke with a start. Something had made a noise in the *skog*. Probably a deer barking, as they do. And then I saw a very strange sight. To my right, the sky was still orange from the sunset. But at the same time, to my left, the sky was already a deep orange from the sunrise. I could see the sunset and the sunrise at the same time.

Only in Sweden, I thought to myself.

And fell back asleep in my hammock.

*

With midsummer out of the way, the summer itself cranked up another gear or two. Still somewhat to our surprise, as it was Sweden after all, in clear blue skies almost unfussed with jet trails or cloud, the sun was out on most days and it even got pretty hot.

In fact I knew exactly what the temperature was thanks to my now expanding collection of thermometers, and it reached 27 °C on two consecutive days. Which, given that the sun was now up until almost midnight, meant a lot of hot sunshine and a lot of suntan cream.

But suntan cream wasn't the only cream to be seen in abundance in Sweden during those hot weeks.

One thing we had already noticed about Swedes – and about men in particular, or so it seemed – was that they loved ice cream. Especially when the sun was out.

It was quite normal to see an incredibly shiny, brand new Audi pull up outside a little shop and for a smartly dressed sales rep or similar to get out and dash into the shop, only to come back five minutes later with an ice cream in a cone. Usually, the ice cream would be bordering on the mountainous and the cone – often locally made – would be far too small.

Sometimes we would sit and watch, from a discreet distance, to see if the thing would melt or collapse with a plop onto the rep's Armani suit. Yet, strangely, it never did. Clearly Swedes knew how to handle ice cream.

We mentioned this one day to Carina, the woman in the shop, and she told us that there was an old fishing trawler moored up in the nearby port of Karlshamn which had been converted into an 'ice cream boat'. A sort of nautical ice cream parlour. She promised us that if we wanted an ice cream that was the place to visit.

The idea appealed. Hugely. After all, it was summer, and we hadn't yet given ourselves a proper day off by the sea. So on one exceptionally warm day we drove down to the coast to visit Karlshamn and take a look at the ice cream boat.

The drive to Karlshamn, which took about an hour, was almost entirely through forest.

The road was wide, new and we had it almost to ourselves. Once again it felt like driving was intended to be. Sun, beautiful scenery and an empty road. This despite the fact that Karlshamn was the only town of any size for about 40 miles in any direction.

As we approached the edge of the town, one particular piece of industry must have been some sort of chicken preparation plant because the smell was definitely that of battery farmed chickens. It was the kind of smell that, once you knew it, you couldn't mistake it. And it was pretty off-putting.

One unusual thing we had noticed about Sweden and about Swedish coastal towns in particular was that there were often surprisingly ugly industrial buildings right on the sea front – a thing which passes seemingly unnoticed by the Swedes themselves. Whether this was because they regarded industry as an inherently attractive thing or whether they were perhaps taught to admire industrial architecture during lessons at school, we couldn't say. But we had certainly noticed the same phenomenon throughout the country and it still surprised us, even if it didn't stir the Swedish.

Having gotten past the rancid chicken smell, however, and looking in the opposite direction to the ugliest of those industrial buildings, Karlshamn itself was quite a pretty town with a good mixture of houses and shops. An old fishing port, we assumed, it was now a quiet town which clearly relied a lot on summer tourism.

The ice cream boat was there too. Right down on the harbour. Just as Carina had promised. And so we climbed aboard.

The old boat certainly had some character. And with a prow (or stern, I could never remember which was which) very high above the water, walking up the old wooden decking was quite an achievement. It was a shame that the boat was also moored directly below some large grey concrete buildings, but it did have a canopy to protect passengers and ice creams from the sun, which extended right across the deck and so, once seated, you couldn't see the industry without craning your neck. In fact all you could really see was the bright sparkling gleam coming from the water down below.

I bagged a table and a couple of chairs on the water side of the ship and Emma went to the counter to buy the ice creams.

As I sat there, a large pink Swedish woman came past with the biggest ice creams I had ever seen. Two of them. Each piled precariously high. She walked past me and sat at a table just behind me. And I was more than a little surprised to see that she was on her own.

Clearly Emma and I had been right; the Swedish loved their ice cream! Emma returned with our own, only slightly smaller helpings, and we ploughed determinedly through them but had to admit defeat long before they were finished.

After the battle of the ice cream, we decided to take a short drive around the town, to have a look at the coast there.

The Baltic coastline was almost completely unknown territory to us. We had seen it briefly in the autumn when we were looking for a house to buy, and we had seen it in the winter when we visited Kalmar. But neither brief visit had prepared us for what was such a beautiful and almost completely unspoiled coastline.

We found ourselves just a few kilometres outside of central Karlshamn and – though we had to pinch ourselves to believe it – we were still in both the suburbs of the town and, in fact, still in Sweden. For it didn't look like Sweden. It looked like Greece. It looked like a Greek island.

The coast was rocky but edged with low hills and cliffs. These hills were partly bare and partly covered with conifers – which really gave it that Mediterranean look and feel. The sea sparkled under a clear blue sky. And the water was crystal clear.

Out in the bay there were a few islands, some wooded and mysterious looking, one or two low and flat and seemingly nothing but bare rock.

"It's absolutely beautiful", said Emma.

And so it was.

We clambered down a few rocks onto a small beach, then crossed that and walked along an almost deserted pathway which followed the line of the cliffs.

We sat on a little wooden jetty and got changed for a dip.

It took a while to summon up the nerve to get into the water. After all, this was the Baltic. Wouldn't it be ice cold? We had seen parts of it freeze over in the winter.

In fact we were in for quite a shock. The water was both warmer than the English Channel and virtually salt-free. The clarity also made for fantastic underwater swimming, and for several hours we were lost to the pleasures of crabs, seaweed, sunshine and sunbathing.

It all seemed very remote from the country that had been under so much snow just a few months beforehand.

*

At the end of June, the gate returned to haunt me.

Following my internet order, it was now overdue by a week or so, and so I decided to go back online and check with the supplier as to when I might expect to receive it.

The news wasn't good.

Apparently there had been a mistake at the time of the order because the site had told me that yes, definitely, this gate was available in Sweden. Whereas it now turned out that it wasn't. At least, not normally so.

I was a little bit miffed about this, having already paid for it and having expected it to have already arrived. But I pressed on and asked the chat desk what they meant by "not normally so".

The woman on there told me that, in this case, as something of a 'show gate', so to speak, they were prepared to deliver to me in Sweden as they wanted to both honour their commitment and expand further into the Scandinavian market.

It sounded good to me. So I asked when I could now expect delivery.

Once again, the woman was very helpful and she told me that it would be dispatched later that very week. I would have it before the end of the month.

It was good news and I admired German efficiency at that moment in time almost as much as I had been admiring different aspects of Swedish efficiency over the last six months or so.

It would be inaccurate to say that I then spent the remainder of June sitting looking out of the window waiting for the arrival of my new gate. I assumed it would be delivered by a medium sized van.

Inaccurate. Yes. But only up to a point.

In truth I did find myself sitting outside, in the sunshine, with my laptop and working, and feeling more or less ready to jump up at the sound of the aforementioned van. Not exactly like a coiled spring, but not far off.

Fortunately the Germans were good to their word. Had they not been, I could easily have spent the rest of that summer hanging around waiting for the delivery. But one Friday, the last Friday in June, I heard an engine, saw a truck and sprang up ready to welcome my gate to Sweden.

The truck was big. Huge, in fact.

And it was German.

That did make me feel special. It had come all that way, just for me.

The driver jumped down out of the cab, smiling. And presented me with a piece of paper. A receipt for my gate.

We then went around the back of the truck and he opened the large double doors.

And there, occupying pretty much the whole of the rear of the vast container, was an enormous package.

The driver hopped up into the vehicle and said, in rough English, "Your gate!", which actually sounded more like 'frigate'. And for one horrible moment, I actually imagined that was what was inside the vast package. A new warship.

"My gate?" I said, "All of that package for my gate?"

The driver nodded and began to operate some sort of crane device.

"Just a moment", I said. This was time to double check the receipt. Not the kind of thing I normally did.

And there it was. On the receipt. In black and white. Not just one gate. There were *one hundred* of the things in the truck!

No wonder the German company had decided to ship specially to me. And to make my gate a show gate.

By now Emma was with me, and she spoke a little German.

A short conversation took place and the driver agreed that there had been an error. And with another cheerful smile he headed back to his cab.

"Hang on hang on", I said, "You can offload one of them. I want one gate!"

But no. Apparently that wasn't possible. The driver even made a call to the company but they wouldn't deliver a single gate. It was all or nothing. And so the day ended with my gate, and its 99 companions, all being driven away and setting off south to spend the rest of the summer in a German garden centre.

It was good news in a way, as I would never have found the space to keep or display one hundred garden gates. And the return postage would have been prohibitive. All the same, it still left me gateless in Sweden.

Two months had gone by. Shops had been visited. Heads had been shaken. The internet had delivered. And then taken away again. No one knew where I could buy a gate.

So there was only one thing for it; make my own gate.

The idea of making my own did seem to somehow fit with the frontier-like feel of the country I was now living in. And wasn't that exactly what Edvard had advised me to do? Clearly this was a country where you had to take on new challenges. Even if that did just mean making your own garden gate. And I forgot, quite deliberately, that I had failed my 'O' level in woodwork and that wood and I had never, ever, seen eye-to-eye from that day to this.

I even had the brilliant – to me – idea of re-using the heavy wooden pallets that our pellets were delivered on. (After six months we now had a tidy little pile of these things on our land

and Olof never seemed interested in taking them away or collecting them in the way the milkman used to collect 'empties'.)

And so it was that, for the next four or five days, I cut and measured and nailed and fixed and glued various bits of wood together until the gates started to take shape.

The end result?

A ghastly, lop sided, eyesore of a gate.

Had I hung it at the end of our drive, it was certainly have made a statement: it would have said, in no uncertain terms 'An idiot lives here'.

In the end it took a very short time to dismantle. Far less time than it had taken to construct it. And it would burn nicely on the wood burning stove, once the cold weather returned.

July

By the start of July, I too had developed the almost nervous tick of checking the thermometers and muttering to myself that things were looking up or felt unseasonably hot or cold. As I did it, I knew that all over Sweden other men were doing the same thing. Peering through the window. Going outside to check the bigger gauges. It even began to feel like something you might be quizzed about should you apply for citizenship. A necessary Swedish skill.

I could imagine the questions. What was the coldest day in 2017? How many consecutive days of rainfall were there in June of the same year?

Fortunately I also felt that I now knew most of the answers.

And so it was that, on the 4th of July, coinciding with American independence day, after two weeks without a drop of rain, I noticed that the temperature was a quite staggering 32 °C. A figure we had never expected to see in Sweden.

"We must go down to the sea", I said.

"Where?"

"Karlshamn".

"The ice cream boat again?"

"No", I said emphatically, "for another swim!"

Twenty minutes later and with a packed lunch in the car, we set off for the coast. Or, rather, we planned to set off for the coast.

Not only is Sweden a huge country, about a thousand miles or so from top to bottom, but most of that land is wild. Forests and lakes. It would probably be pretty impractical to police all that space and ask people to keep off it. So, a long time ago, it became accepted that you could go anywhere. Walk on any land. Camp on any land. Swim in any water. Canoe on any water. Collect berries or mushrooms whenever and wherever you wanted.

This law, though not exactly a law more just a custom, is called Allemansrätt (alla-mans-ret) which means, literally, 'Everyone's Right', as in everyone has right of access to the countryside. And it does just what it says on the tin; everyone has virtually unlimited access to nature.

The only land that's out of bounds is land under crops and private gardens. But in the winter, when snow is on the ground, even these exceptions can be walked across.

Coming from the UK, where access to the land is very limited, Allemansrätt seemed heaven-sent. And we had both already taken advantage of it many times by going for long meandering walks without having to consult maps in advance and work out where we could and couldn't go.

Because of Allemansrätt, or maybe just because the country is so big and devoid of people and buildings, but full of trees and all shades of wildlife, Sweden is the sort of country that exudes freedom. A responsible freedom, admittedly, and not a reckless freedom. You can light a fire in the forest, for example, but not during the summer. The ground is tinder dry. And to light a fire, no matter how small, could be disastrous. So you just wouldn't do it anyway. And even if you light one during the cooler damper parts of the year, you must always ensure it is thoroughly and totally extinguished before you leave it. The same applies to things like litter. There is nothing to stop you leaving litter – but it's the last thing on earth that you would ever want to do. The place is virtually unspoiled – so why spoil it?

And that attitude applies across the board.

As part and parcel of that, we had already learned to approach Sweden – and life in Sweden – with a take-it-as-you-find-it attitude. Having a plan is a great idea, but doggedly sticking to it is not. (As I was slowly discovering with the gate!)

It took just over an hour to drive to Karlshamn. And the first part of that drive – before hitting a new, four-lane and almost wholly empty road – was along narrow lanes through the forest, with signs occasionally pointing to a hamlet tucked away deep in the skog.

It was a beautiful day, and we had plenty of time – the sun didn't go down until around 11pm. And so, rather than drive directly to the coast, we decided to more or less meander in the direction of it. If it took two hours, instead of one, that was fine by us.

We had taken similar diversions before. And had discovered very little. Just a few red houses and a lot of forest. But on this day, things turned out a little different.

"Oh", said Emma, who was half-heartedly map reading whilst I drove. "A kilometre or two from here there's a museum, I think. At least, I think it's a museum".

I continued driving and she looked up the 'museum' on her phone.

"Oh yes!" she exclaimed, suddenly. "Let's visit it. It looks really interesting on the internet".

The 'museum' was a left turn, onto a narrow forestry road, a short distance along there, a right turn onto a dirt track, a short distance along there, and then a full stop. The middle of nowhere. With nothing to be seen.

"There it is", said Emma. Opening the car door, getting out and setting off for the 'museum'.

A hundred metres away 'it', as far as I could see, was just a very small cottage. Painted the usual slightly dour Falun red, and sited in a small patch of typically poor land – thin earth and coarse grass covering a rocky soil – and with very little else of note, I wondered how or why this little building was considered a museum.

As we walked up to the cottage, I noticed that the roof seemed to be made of grass. Or perhaps the place had just been neglected so much that grass had taken root up there. If I had been grass, I think I would have found it easier to grow on a roof than on the hard Scandinavian land.

"What is this place?" I asked Emma as I caught up with her.

"Look!" she said, pointing at a sign.

The sign offered a little information as to what the house was. Apparently this was the former home of a shoemaker. And now, preserved, it was a sort of museum.

"Free to enter and not even locked?" I asked.

"Seems so", replied Emma.

That felt a very un-British sort of experience.

We went into the cottage through a rather low door. And that was the moment at which I realised just why the building had been preserved and was considered quite special. The door was low. Very low. And the cottage was tiny. Very tiny. And, once inside, it became apparent why this was the case; the shoemaker had been no more than a metre or so tall. And everything in the house was sized accordingly.

Little Paul's cottage, as the place turned out to be called, was a lovely and wholly unexpected find.

Inside, with very low ceilings, there was a tiny cot-like bed, clothes made for a very small but stylish man, and all the sorts of things you might expect to find in a house. A small table. Tiny chairs. Little wooden clogs. And – laid out just as if Paul was going to come home at any moment – all the tools and materials of the cobbler's trade.

It was wonderful.

Life in that cottage, isolated at it was, must have been far from easy. No electric. No running water. No modern conveniences. Yet without nearby neighbours, surrounded by clean air and a little bit of roughly cleared land, it must also have been utterly tranquil.

And as we left, signing the guest book as we did so, I envied Little Paul his life in that place.

I envied the Swedish too. Little Paul had been dead for over 100 years. But still, in this often hectic modern world, the Swedish felt – rightly – that they could keep this little cottage unlocked, and free to visit, for anyone who had the time or inclination to do so.

The more we trust, the more we are trusted and the better we relate to one another. And just because, from time to time, a rotten apple lets us down, we should then trust all the more – not less. Open up. Not close down.

After Little Paul's house, we set off once more, with the plan being to drive to the coast and have a swim.

But, once again, the free spirits, elves and fairies which must, surely, inhabit the Swedish forest, got the better of us.

Only this time it was a lake.

Being British, neither of us had ever swum in a lake before.

And as we headed for Karlshamn and the rocky Swedish seashore, a sparkling, flashing and utterly enticing glimmer of water took our eye. And Emma – who was now driving – screeched to a stop.

"Look at that water!" she said.

A blue diamond. Glittering in the trees.

"Why don't we go to the lake instead?"

I agreed. It couldn't hurt to take a look. This was Scandinavia, after all. Everyone swam in the lakes and rivers. Not just the sea.

Back home in the UK, for some utterly inexplicable reason, swimming in freshwater of any kind – lakes, rivers, streams, canals, reservoirs – was always frowned upon. These places were death traps. Unsafe. Signs warned swimmers to stay away.

Why were the Swedish waters so different? I had no idea. Did they clean them? Were they all just a few feet deep? Were there lifeguards and security cameras posted all along the shore, and teams of rescue boats ready to emerge at a moment's notice?

No. Of course not. It was that old chestnut of trusting people. And people responding to trust by acting (usually) in a trustworthy manner.

Anyway. We turned the car around and took a narrow track to the lakeside. There were signs along the route, telling us that there was even a campsite nearby, and various facilities.

We finally came to what seemed to be a car park in that there was a P sign and two or three cars drawn up in a large gravelled space amongst tall pine trees. And, taking our swimming stuff with us, we walked towards the campsite.

To our surprise, the campsite itself was rather small and very busy. A dozen or more tents and caravans were crammed into a small area, squeezed in as close to one another as they could be – almost as if they were all members of the same family. Yet some of the cars were German and some were Danish, so the chances that they were all the same family were pretty slight.

We were also surprised at the size and condition of the Swedish caravans. For a country so wealthy, comparatively speaking, and with two homes, a horse and a yacht per family being quite common, clearly the Swedes liked to save money when it came to buying – or perhaps renewing – their caravans.

Most of them were smaller than the Volvos which towed them. And all of them looked like they were taken straight from the film 'Carry on Camping', both in terms of condition and age.

Sneaking up close to one of them, just to look, Emma read a sign which said that the caravan in question was actually a 'Four Season Van'. And, of course Sweden being Sweden, for at least one of those seasons any caravan would need to be pretty well insulated!

"How can they be four seasons?" she laughed, as we walked past a collection of outdoor games for the campers. "They don't look weather proof for the summer, never mind temperatures well below freezing".

The beach – or, to be specific, the beach designated for the campsite – was also fairly small. But clean. And covered with very soft sand.

Elsewhere, around the lake, here and there, there were other beaches and places to access the water. We could see some of them – and people using them – from where we were. But we didn't mind having a small beach and sharing it with the campers. If anything it was rather nice to be in the middle of a forest surrounded by sun-tanned and tanning Scandinavians and Germans.

Emma and I quickly got changed and headed for the water.

There were two long and rather shaky looking wooden jetties leading out into the lake. And there were a handful of people sitting on them and, at the ends, one or two jumping in and out of the water. We reached the end of the nearest jetty and hesitated.

Our first ever freshwater dip. Neither of us were sure what to expect.

How deep was the water? Would there be mud or stones below it? Would it be warm or cold?

Of course there was only one way to find out. And so that was what we did. We took hold of each other's hands. And jumped.

Surprisingly the water was very mild. Like a bath which had been run perhaps an hour beforehand. And it was deep, too. No obvious bottom could be found before swimming a few metres towards the shore. But it was also quite wonderful. Not least because, and pretty obviously so, it was freshwater. Not salty. And so when a lot of it went up your nose, it was fine.

It was our first real experience of just why it was that Sweden was considered to be such a nature lover's paradise.

We spent an hour or so in that lake. In and out. Lying in the sun. On the jetty. Jumping in. And it was really quite a treat. And we promised ourselves that, from now on, whenever it was sunny we would take a quick dip in a lake. After all, they were all over the place. Whereas the sea was an hour or so's drive away.

Finally as it began to turn a little cooler, and we got hungry, we noticed the smell of something, cooking, food, coming from one of the cabins of the campsite. And even from the beach we could see that it was a cafe of some sort.

So we towelled ourselves dry and went across to see if there was anything we would want to risk trying, not having had much joy thus far at eating out in Sweden.

Of course being a little campsite cafe, there were the usual things like pizzas and ice cream. Nothing that really interested us. But they also did waffles (a sign above the counter actually said the cafe was a 'Vaffelstuga' or waffle cottage) and Emma decided to try one of those.

Then I noticed an old chap, who must have been at least 80 years old and who had spent most of the afternoon swimming in the lake, order a thing called a 'Kroppkaka' the translation of which I couldn't manage. It looked unusual. And, perhaps foolishly, I was always keen to try anything which looked a little different.

So as Emma ordered her waffle, with honey and cream topping, I asked the woman serving what a 'kroppkaka' was. And in fluent English she explained that it was mashed potato, filled with minced pork and onions and served with a big puddle of melted butter and lingonberry jam.

Emma heard this and pulled a face. And I almost hesitated at ordering one, because I had tasted Swedish jam a few times already – and it was horribly sugary. Far too little fruit and far too much sugar. They also had a tendency to put too much salt on everything. So, all in all, it really sounded like a recipe for a disaster. But I ordered one anyway.

"You're crazy", said Emma. "It's bound to be awful!"

I nodded. "Maybe the sun has gone to my head", I laughed.

Five minutes later, we were both seated at a heavy wooden picnic table, about to try some more Swedish food.

To our amazement, this time – the first time – it was actually pretty good. The waffle and honey was sweet, of course, but Emma was adamant that it wasn't too sweet. Just right. And as for the kroppkaka, it was fine. Weird. Yes. But fine. The potato went well with the meat, went well with the onion, went well with the butter. And if the lingonberry jam had been a bit less sugary, the whole thing could have scored an 8 out of 10.

The only thing that was missing to complete a happy and spontaneous summer's day was a pint or two of good rough cider or, at least, a glass of red wine. Sadly neither was available. And the 'Pripps Blue' lager, which the cafe did sell, was somewhat less palatable than the water in the lake.

Still. We had no right to complain.

*

Around mid-July, during a busy afternoon dozing in a hammock, my phone beeped with a message. It was from Jack the Canadian sculptor, who we had first met on Walpurgis Night at the end of April. At first I wasn't quite sure what he wanted, as the message he left for me seemed to be a bit garbled. So I called him back and asked him what the problem was. Because one of us, probably me, was clearly a little confused.

"You want me to contact the BBC?" I asked him.

"No, no, no", he said, "I have been contacted by the BBC and now I don't know what to do".

"About..."

"The studio", said Jack, "I don't have one at the moment. That's what I've been saying. I did have one. But mine burned down a couple of years back after a particularly heavy night on the bourbon with a few of the guys. But, now, if I could just get one, a studio I mean, even temporarily, then they, the BBC, would be able to come and see me, and my stuff. In a studio. Without one, I don't know what to do. I don't think they'll come unless I can find one..."

I didn't work for the BBC. I had never worked for them. And although I was in the process of converting a small outhouse into an artist's studio, it wasn't ready yet and it was too small for sculpture in any case. And I told Jack that. But, at the same time, I did feel a bit guilty, because when Emma and I had called around to his, that night in April, we had talked about art and I had mentioned to him that I knew of some artists, locally, who were based in a re-furbished factory building not far from Kalmar. Which was true. I had also told him that the factory was a wonderful place to have an art studio. All those high ceilings and big windows and space. Which may or may not have been true. I hadn't yet been there. But when the bourbon was flowing merrily back on Walpurgis Night, that detail hadn't seemed to matter. Clearly Jack's memory of that evening was better than mine, and now he was calling me to see if I could help him out.

We talked for a while longer and Jack explained that the BBC were doing a series about how the 2008 recession was still – all these years later – affecting the art world in various ways, and they had seen some of his stuff from that period online and that now they wanted to come over and visit him and include some of his work in the programme.

"So where do you work now, then?" I asked him. He was an artist and he been in Sweden for some years, so I figured he must already have some space set aside for working.

"Well, to be honest at the moment all I have is a big shed that I use for storage. Since my own place burned down I've worked outdoors. In the summer. In the winter I have to stop work. And you've seen my place. It isn't that big. No room inside for sculpting. It wouldn't pass for a studio on the television".

"So you want me to help you find a studio?" I said.

"Yes", said Jack, "I was thinking, maybe that factory you mentioned...."

"And when do the BBC want to see your stuff?"

"In two weeks' time", came the answer.

I wasn't sure that I could help but I agreed to try. And as soon as Jack had hung up I called my friends at the factory near Kalmar.

I had known Anders since our university days. He had been a foreign student, in Wales, for one year. Part of an exchange scheme. And I had met him a few times on some long walks which a group of us took in the Welsh hills. We had got on well and somehow we had even stayed in touch – albeit quite distantly. He was a surfer. And he looked like a surfer. Tall, square shouldered, handsome and usually bronze coloured. His partner, Linda, I had only met once or twice. But she was very much the female equivalent of Anders. Also tall, tanned and good looking. Anders was busy when I called, working with a glass blowing furnace, but Linda was there. We said hello, I told her very roughly what I was doing and why. And then I mentioned Jack and his need for a studio. She sounded enthusiastic enough about the idea and thought it would be great publicity to have the BBC visit the factory in Kalmar. And as time was short, she suggested we went over as soon as possible to see the place.

I thanked Linda and checked whether either she or Anders would still be there for a few more hours that day. They would.

I knew Jack was in a hurry so I called him back straight away, and told him to get his boots on. And a few hours later we arrived at the factory in Kalmar.

Things were going very smoothly and I felt that maybe I had missed my calling in life as a 'fixer' or something like that. Sweden was obviously a 'can-do' type of country.

As we arrived at the factory-cum-studio, a former glassblowing works now coming back to life as a centre for artists of all types, Anders was there to meet us. We said hello, I introduced Jack and we went into the building, where Linda was poring over some diagrams on an oversized drawing board.

Although back at university, as far as I could recall, Anders had studied history, today he was a pretty successful self-employed graphic designer. Linda too. She worked with Anders and helped to get him major advertising contracts, the most recent for no less a company than Scania – the huge haulage company.

And as Anders took Jack around the building to show him the studios, I sat and talked with Linda about their work.

Some of their jobs, such as the one for Scania but also another which they had recently completed for Audi, were clearly worth a good deal of money. And business trips, all expenses paid, for both Anders and Linda to New York or Geneva were now fairly typical events.

As Linda told me about all of this, I noticed that she did so without any suggestion of boasting or even pride. It was just like that. Matter of fact. They were well educated. They were Swedish. They worked together. They worked hard. Why should it not be like that?

It was something I had noticed before. A strange but extremely refreshing thing about Sweden, and Swedes in general, was that there was little or no sign of social status. If you earned a lot of money, it was certainly not something you boasted about. In fact Swedes were almost apologetic when it came to money – especially if they were comfortably well off.

No doubt in parts of Stockholm and perhaps Gothenburg there were such distinctions. The tower blocks on the edge of the cities were where immigrants and the poorer Swedes lived. And from time to time, life on those estates could be pretty tough – according to what we picked up now and then from the news or a newspaper. By contrast, some of the islands in the Stockholm archipelago were hideously expensive and very exclusive. The kind of place where the former members of Abba might buy a home.

But out here, away from such extremes, it was often hard to tell if someone was rich or poor, working, studying or simply retired. Everyone seemed to drive Volvos. Lots of people seemed to own a second home somewhere else in the country. Owning and riding horses or owning a boat was considered quite normal. And more or less every house was detached.

I asked Linda whether there was enough work for her and Anders to employ someone else. She looked surprised.

"Yes, of course", she said, "We have two others who work for us and we would like to recruit maybe another. But, sadly, the taxes get a little high".

That was certainly no exaggeration. I had read somewhere that the total tax take in Sweden was something like 60% or more. Ouch. But then, it did seem to contribute to a fairer, calmer and more affordable society. So maybe it was a price well worth paying.

After about 20 minutes, Anders and Jack came back and we all sat for a short while and shared a few glasses of something very strong and completely clear that Linda produced from an ancient looking cupboard.

As I was driving, I limited myself to just one glass – I didn't ask what the drink was, but it had a potency very similar to poitin, which I had drunk a few times in my youth. And it wouldn't have surprised me at all to discover that Swedes made their own version of that Irish rocket fuel.

It had been a long day for Linda and Anders, because artists or not, like most Swedes they had begun work at 8 am. So I promised them that we would meet up soon, together with Emma, and go for a meal or drink. Anders said that that was a great idea and told me that he knew a good place to eat on the coast. I hoped it wasn't the same place Emma and I had visited in Kalmar.

"Well?" I asked Jack as we drove away, "Was the studio any good?"

Jack was glum. "No. It was nice. Very nice. You know how things are over here. But the studios are really too small and the whole place just too clean and tidy. It didn't have the right arty sort of feeling. No big windows. More like a design office. A studio for drawing. Design. You know. Everything was so clean and new!"

I did know what he meant, and as drove back home, I promised to do what I could to help.

Over the course of the next few days, Emma, Jack and I searched various sources to try and find something a little less Scandinavian and a bit more Bohemian.

It turned out that lots of former industrial or agricultural buildings, across the whole of southern Sweden, had been brought back to life by being converted into offices, studios, small industrial units or even flats.

And as we looked into some of these a bit further, what surprised me most of all was the location of many of these buildings. Often, in former times, industry in Sweden had been situated in the forest or in a village of no more than perhaps ten or twenty houses. I was more used to seeing industry concentrated in large towns and cities, and this more rural approach seemed a little strange.

But so it was that we saw a huge industrial mill, standing quite alone in the countryside and which had once employed almost a thousand people. And other similar oddities. The buildings were often quite wonderful; one was a four-storey timber building with literally dozens of windows. Another looked for all the world more like a hunting lodge than a place of oil and toil. We saw another former industrial site which was now host to the biggest Christmas fair in Sweden. It wasn't the kind of place that Jack wanted; he wanted something "more urban", but Emma and I made a mental note to visit the place again when the Christmas fair was on. It was such a lovely site.

In short the whole experience opened our eyes up more to the industrial power that had been – and to a large extent still was – Sweden. This was a country where minerals, water and other resources were exploited in situ. It was a manufacturing country. And, of course, much of those natural reserves were the source of its wealth.

We didn't find a suitable studio for Jack, however.

Everything we saw was small or too modern or both. Great places for new business start-ups. No traffic jams, fast internet and a rural setting. Moose on the lawn almost guaranteed. But nothing was the classic artist's studio such as the three of us envisaged it. And with the BBC now phoning him every day, Jack was getting desperate. He needed to tell them that they could come over, that he would have a studio to show them, that his work would be there. And he was too honest a chap to fake it.

Finally the whole matter came to a head. A friend of Emma's knew someone who had a friend in Växjö who was, in turn, a sculptor. We were given a phone number. And we made a last ditch call.

"My studio, yes, yes, you can come and see. Yes, it is in an old building here in the city. Big, yes. Draughty really. It can be too cold to work".

It sounded ideal.

We telephoned Jack but got no answer. We drove round to his house in the village. He wasn't in.

So Emma and I raced off in the car to Växjö to see the sculptor's studio for ourselves.

It was perfect. A large high-ceilinged space in an old red-brick factory building. Big windows. A bare concrete floor, whitewashed walls and big searching spotlights in the ceiling.

We said we'd take it. And we drove back as fast as we could to find Jack.

We found him sitting on the doorstep of his home enjoying a cup of coffee and a little bit of warm sunshine.

We told him our news. But we didn't get the response that we expected.

"Damn", said Jack, "Damn it. I had to call the BBC this morning to tell them that they couldn't come. I told them I had nothing to show them".

"Call them back", said Emma, "Tell them you can do it".

He did. But the BBC had already made other plans.

So, in the end, our sculptor friend missed out on his big chance of publicity. But he wasn't too bothered. Jack was a pretty sanguine fellow most of the time. And we had had quite an eye-opening experience discovering all sorts of places and buildings and bits of Swedish history that we would otherwise have known nothing about.

*

After my failure to help Jack become a TV star and world-renowned artist, and because the sun was still out – for the umpteenth week on the trot – I needed to retire to my hammock again and recover my strength.

Prior to this summer, I had never even seen a hammock except for in old films about pirates and the like. But one day in April, as the big stores began to parade their wares for the summer season, Emma had spotted what turned out to be a wonderful bargain: hammocks. Thick, multi-coloured, and presumably strong enough to support a Swede – who all tended to be larger than either of us – we couldn't believe the price. Each hammock cost the equivalent of only ten pounds sterling. Needless to say we had bought a couple.

We also had the ideal place for fixing up two hammocks.

Buying Swedish property seems to consist of buying a house, naturally enough, and at least a half dozen assorted sheds and outhouses. No home is complete unless each generation has erected a robust shed.

Our property was no exception to that. And some of those outbuildings were both attractive and useful. One, in particular, I was in the process of converting into a small guest cottage and painting studio.

Not all of them were in the same category, however. Every house we walked past seemed to have an ugly cousin somewhere or other in the garden. An overly large or tumbledown shack. A small thing that would struggle to serve as a dog kennel. A hideously painted and hopelessly sited shed, something rotting, or – as was the case with some of these strange buildings on our land – poorly designed outhouses that were more tatty old windows than structure, and which made old square Volvos look like Italian master classes of style and design.

We had they two like that. And they had to go.

And they had gone. Back in the winter. When chain sawing was the only way to keep warm outside.

However, one of these ghastly affairs had been constructed around a metal framework, almost like a climbing frame. And at the very last minute, rather than angle-grinding the frame into small pieces and taking it to the recycling yard, I had decided to keep it.

It was ugly, yes. But nothing that a coat of good paint wouldn't fix. And besides, I could encourage plants to climb up it. And – thanks to Emma's eye for a bargain – it made a superb framework on which to hang a few hammocks. Right next to the house. With a great view across our garden and land.

And that was where I spent the last day of July. It was too hot to move. So with a book, drink, laptop and one or two other items, I lay in the hammock and dutifully fell asleep.

It was much cooler by the time I awoke, a beautiful early dusk. The sky a fine turquoise colour with just a few streaks of pink.

"Hello", said Emma. "Here you are. I didn't come looking for you before because I needed you out of the way so I could finish that rush job on the laptop. Are you OK?"

"Yes", I said, yawning and stretching. "I guess I must have dozed off".

Emma sat in the other hammock and for a while we just chatted about the sky and the forest and the peace and quiet. When, suddenly, there was what can only be described as a low bellowing sound. From very nearby.

"What the hell's that?" she said.

I had no idea. And we both looked in the direction of the gate – or where the gate was going to be, at the end of the drive.

Needless to say the noise was a moose. It came tearing across our garden, in as much as a knock-kneed moose can tear. And we both laughed.

Only in rural Sweden could such tranquillity be shattered by a bellowing moose!

Then we saw why the moose was running. And what had made it bellow.

A second moose, much bigger, with antlers the size of branches, was giving chase.

We stood and watched the two of them disappear into the forest, then I went indoors to fetch out two glasses and a nice bottle of red wine. It seemed an ideal way to end the hottest month of the year.

August

The first of August marks the beginning of a whole month of school holidays – in the UK. For most children, it is the best month of the year. The only one during which they never have to attend school.

It isn't like that in Sweden. Everyone goes back to work in mid-August. The schools re-open in mid-August.

And that isn't due to any kind of mean-spiritedness on behalf of the Swedish state. There's no deliberate attempt to snip summer in half. It is rather that summer, typically, ends at or about mid-August. The back half of the month usually – but not always – resembling what we Brits would think of as September, in terms of weather.

We had told that to our next visitors. In fact we had told them so deliberately, with the idea being that they would visit during that back half of August, because they would find travel and so forth to be cheaper. And with two children, and not the most well paid of jobs, it would have made sense for them to take our advice. But they had seen it otherwise – they wanted to be in Sweden during the 'proper' holidays. To see the ice cream boat open, to see people on the beach and so forth. And it was their holiday after all. So we didn't say no. In any case, it did make sense to visit in early August, just in case this was one of the years that September arrived early.

As it was, much in keeping with a great deal of June and most of July, when they arrived on the third of August, Sweden was on its very best behaviour. The sky overhead was deep blue, once again untroubled by aircraft contrails, and the temperature was in the very high 20s, with more forecast for the week ahead.

"Wow", said Kate as she stretched out in one of our hammocks, her pale skin clearly in need of some sunlight. "We had no idea Sweden was like this. So hot. So sunny. We've packed at least one case full of just waterproofs and jumpers!"

Emma laughed. She was sitting at a fold away table and working, albeit a little half-heartedly, on her laptop. "It isn't Scotland", she said.

"I know what you mean, though", I added. "We were the same. You feel that being northerly means cold and wet. But here, mostly, it doesn't".

Mark, Kate's partner, had taken their two children, Gregory and Lisa, up to the village shop to buy them some ice cream. I had offered to go with him, but he was very adamant that he was going to be brave and try out some holiday Swedish at the first possible opportunity.

"You won't get a chance", I laughed. "I've been here for more than six months and I've barely said ten words in Swedish. As soon as they see you're British, they'll switch to English".

Emma and I had shown him the bridle path, and he had gone off with the kids – first sousing them and himself with Mygga.

Mark and Kate were both teachers, committed to their work and always doing the best for the kids in their class. But we knew from things they both said, from time to time, that things weren't easy in their profession, and that they weren't getting easier. There were cuts, shortages, a lack of discipline, too much paperwork and the government kept moving the goalposts.

There was something else too, which both Emma and I knew, but didn't volunteer. It just came out in a roundabout sort of way during our conversation whilst Mark was up at the shop.

"And they're teachers?" asked Kate, incredulously.

"Yes", replied Emma.

"And they really have a yacht?"

Emma nodded.

A few months earlier, sitting having a coffee in the village shop with Carina one day, we had gotten into a chat with two Swedes who were teachers in nearby Växjö. They both loved their jobs.

And – so they told us and we had no reason to doubt them – they felt cared for and stress free. Mostly stress free anyway.

It also turned out that they had a home, here in the village, and a second in the forest nearer to the sea. And they regularly took holidays abroad and even had a yacht.

And that, they assured us, was pretty standard for two teachers or, even, two of anyone if they lived in the countryside, away from the big cities, and both worked full time.

Kate couldn't believe it. And we both tried hard to change the subject by pointing out how bad the food was, and how the midges stung and how it was such a long winter... but by the time Mark and the kids came back, only just reaching the end of their huge ice creams, Kate was already on the laptop looking up 'How to move to Sweden'.

"Is it true you've got a couple of kayaks?" asked Mark, sitting down and finally finishing his ice cream cone. It had taken him the whole walk back from the village to eat it.

I nodded. "Yes. Emma spotted them in one of the big out of town shops. She's got an eye for that sort of thing. They're only plastic but they work".

Mark looked up at the sky. It was beautiful.

"I don't suppose we could take them out for an hour, could we?"

Neither Emma nor I needed much persuading. We were up to date with our work. And it was too nice to sit here and miss a trip to the sea.

So it was that about an hour or so later, with two cars and one trailer loaded with boats and paddles, we all arrived at the sea.

No sooner had we got there than we realised that our life jackets – of which we only had two – were both adult sized. Emma and I immediately began to worry about this, but Mark and Kate were much more 'Swedish' in their outlook.

"The kids will be fine", Mark insisted. "They can both swim like fish and, anyway, I'm sure someone will rescue them if anything goes wrong".

There were plenty of people on the beach and lying on the rocks of the cove, and the sea – which was crystal clear at this point – was both warm and shallow. It was also a tideless bay. So we took Mark at his word and dragged the kayaks down to the water's edge.

"How are we going to work this?" Emma asked. "Do you two want to go out, one each, with Gregory on one boat and Lisa on the other?"

Neither Gregory nor Lisa were keen on that idea. "No. We want to go out by ourselves".

Emma and I left them to it.

And after a few minutes of negotiating, Mark and Kate came up to where we were both sitting, the two kids already paddling furiously out into the bay.

"Are you sure this is going to be OK?" I asked. By now Gregory was already a few hundred metres from the shore.

"They'll be fine", said Kate, lying back in the sun. "Anyway, it'll be easier for us to move to Sweden if they paddle away and get lost!"

The children were clearly having a great time. The sea was waveless. Flat calm. They took the kayaks out and brought them back. Took them out a way again and came back. It was as if the 'freedom' of Sweden had possessed them just like it had their parents. And it was lovely to see.

Eventually Gregory paddled ashore and came up to where we were sitting, Lisa following not far behind.

"Oh, I've got to go and have a go", said Kate, getting up. And both she and Mark jogged down to the beach and hopped onto the little boats.

"God, they both look so much healthier already", said Emma quietly to me as she passed sandwiches to the kids.

It was true. 48 hours in Sweden had taken several years off each of them. But, then, I suppose that happens on most holidays, which is why we should all take one whenever we can.

All the same, younger looking or not, neither Kate nor Mark could handle the kayaks as well as their children, and both ended up falling overboard and into the water.

"It was so warm", said Kate as she came back, reaching for a towel. "When I tipped over I had a horrible thought that it was going to be ice cold".

"It's like Greece!" said Mark as he scoffed the last sandwich. "I can't believe it!"

As forecast, the next few days saw yet more beautiful blue skies filled with a brilliant warm yellow sun. We did the sea again, the ice cream boat and had a swim in the lake. It was summer, after all, and they were on holiday. Besides, there wasn't a great deal more on offer. There were a few stately homes that were open to the public, there were a few museums and things like that, but in the main, Sweden was for nature. For the outdoor life.

Finally it did turn a little cloudier – although still completely dry – and Kate asked the children if they would like to go for a walk in the forest. The skog. Neither of them seemed very keen on the idea until Emma suggested they also take the opportunity to pick berries.

"Berries?" said Lisa. "Strawberries?"

Sweden was a country that was full of strawberries. There were billions of them. But these were wild things with an odd flavour, and tiny, not the sort of fruit that Lisa had in mind.

"No", said Emma. "Not strawberries. Better than that. Blueberries and redberries! The forest is full of them at this time of year."

And so it was, that – once more and very wisely soaked in Mygga, the anti-mosquito roll on – we all set off into the forest to collect lingonberries and bilberries.

Although the season for these two fruit was short, Sweden was famous for the former. Small, tight and tart, dark red lingonberries were to be found throughout the country – free of charge! – growing in the forest. And thanks to Allemansrätt everyone had the right to gather them.

Bilberries were even more plentiful, however. And to collect these, a specially designed plastic scoop had been invented. This was a little bit like a cross between a dustpan and a comb, and you swept the scoop through the low-lying bilberry bush, half-filling it every time. Of course the scoop also caught leaves and twigs, and these had to be separated from the bilberries. But this was easily done by emptying the lot into a bucket of clean water once back home. The twigs and leaves floated, the berries didn't.

Collecting hoards of wild berries was a joy. Not only because it meant meandering through the wild forest and 'getting away from it all', but also because – as you went along with your scoop and bucket or bag – you could eat as many of the things as you wanted!

And, once your back began to ache – which, invariably it did, and which was one of the best reasons to take children along on a berry hunt – you could just find a little clearing and sit in the sun and watch the clouds drift by overhead.

What could be nicer?

The only snag – as Mark soon found out – was that the 'sitting in the sun' part also included 'avoiding the giant ants'. The first time he had a rest, he forgot to do this, and was soon itching and hopping about. Fortunately, for him, he had narrowly avoided their main nest; a four feet high pile of twigs and stuff, which – if disturbed or broken – could have been really quite unpleasant.

"It's so dry out here", said Kate, at one point. "All these desiccated pieces of wood. And the moss. All dry. Like tinder".

"And the boulders", Mark added. "It's like a cold climate jungle. A real wilderness".

"It is like that", Kate agreed. "It must be dangerous. I mean if you fell and broke an ankle. There's no one out here to hear you. And in the winter..."

Emma and I agreed. It was a much harsher environment than we had expected it to be. Even if the bears and wolves were a way to the north of here, just the land itself was dangerous. The fire risk was huge. And as Kate had noticed, if you did have an accident, you would struggle to find help.

"Are there snakes?" Gregory asked, with a worried expression.

"Only little ones". Emma lied. The truth was that there were actually very many adders in Sweden – we had even seen some in the garden. And they were big, chunky and bad tempered looking. But it wasn't the time to tell a child that.

We walked a little further, collected more fruit and then, having been out in the skog for at least three hours, we all went back to the house – via the village shop and the ice cream counter – with enough berries to eat now, tomorrow, for the rest of their holiday and also to put quite a few away in the freezer for the winter.

"Won't the animals go hungry?" Lisa asked, when she saw how many berries we had collected.

"Not really", Emma replied. "The forest is so big, so very very big, that people only gather a tiny amount of the berries. All the rest are eaten by the deer".

Mark, Kate and their two children were leaving in a few days' time. But they'd had, they assured us, both the most relaxing holiday of their lives and something of an eye-opening experience.

"It makes us wonder", said Kate one afternoon as we sat around in the hammocks, the sun once more beating down from a clear Scandinavian sky. "Why are we soldiering on in the UK, when we could move somewhere like this? Everyone speaks English. The houses aren't even expensive".

Emma and I wondered the same thing. Not just about Kate and Mark but about very many people in Britain.

Of course the UK, like everywhere, like everything, everyone, had its upsides. And its downsides. Nowhere was perfect. Nothing was perfect. It was a question of finding the things that offered more upsides than downsides.

"I suppose, in a way, we had kind of imagined that moving abroad was something that only pensioners did. Or wealthy people", Kate continued.

I laughed. "I'm not quite that old yet. And I've hardly ever had two brass farthings to rub together".

"We're lucky though", said Emma. "Without children, I suppose it makes it easier for us to take a gamble. And if it hadn't paid off, we'd be able to try again. With kids, it's always going to be harder".

A short while later, on what was now an absolutely scorchingly hot day, easily 32° C or a bit more, we were all in the cars, windows down, and driving along empty roads towards the village of Tingsryd.

Tingsryd is a pretty village. Largish, with some industry, but still a village. It is situated on what, by Swedish standards, would be considered a small lake, but which is actually quite a reasonable size. (The largest lake in Sweden is about the same size as the county of Devon, in England. But there are very many 'smaller' ones which are still big by any ordinary measure!)

For some reason, perhaps because the lake at Tingsryd is very open, and lies immediately south of the village, with the sun directly above the water, the light just there is really quite special. It has a coastal feel, despite being 40 km or so inland. And on a dark winter's day, it's worth visiting just for the extra intensity of light.

But we were going there today, not for the lake, or the light, or anything like that, but because the streets were closed off for the largest – or one of the largest – annual markets in southern Sweden.

Normally held at the end of July, this year, for some reason, the market had been moved to mid-August. And, according to the official website, having been held for over 100 years, and with over 300 stalls, it now attracted in the region of 40,000 visitors over the course of two days. 40,000 may not sound all that many, but when you remember that the population of Sweden is only 10 million, it is more or less the equivalent of 250,000 visitors to a two-day street market in the UK. And that, by any measure, it quite a lot.

To our surprise, although we were slowly getting used to the concept, car parking was easy and, at least where we parked, free.

The heat, however, was anything but 'easy'. And in Tingsryd itself, even though I didn't have one of my thermometers with me, we all reckoned the temperature had risen to something in the mid-30s. It was very, very hot.

Sadly that heat, combined with the crowds filling the narrow village streets, made for a less enjoyable time than it might otherwise have been. And after just an hour or so, pushing through people to look at any more stalls was out of the question.

We were also a bit disappointed, as the majority of stalls – at least this year – seemed to just be selling modern clothing. T-shirts with garish colours and prints. And there were only a few stalls with hand-made goods or antiques and bric-a-brac.

Nevertheless, Mark and Kate bought a small hand-painted wooden box, which looked very old, and Gregory bought a little wooden Dalarna horse, a traditional Swedish gift, which he was very pleased with.

Finally, we decided that it was once more time for an ice cream. Eating one outside would have been nicer, but the queues were long and, after just a short while in Sweden, we had already gotten used to never having to queue. So instead we went into one of the shops, which we'd seen many adverts for in the local papers, describing itself as established way back and selling everything you could want. A department store. Given our experiences so far in Sweden, Emma and I doubted that this was true. It seemed all the more unlikely as the population of Tingsryd was probably only a few hundred when the market wasn't on.

Sure enough, the inside of the shop was, once more, soviet like. A functional collection of spaces with poor lighting and 1970s lino and decor, the shelves stacked high with all kinds of things that, generally, you don't tend to need. Exactly the same sort of stuff that Woolworths once sold – and which helped it to go out of business.

There was, however, a cafe. Up a staircase which, in itself, looked like it had been removed from a Woolworth's store and shipped intact to Sweden. The whole place had a time-slip like feel to it. We had definitely gone back to the 1970s.

Because most people were outside in the heat, looking at the T-shirts, the self-service cafe was largely empty. The cakes were tiny – and no doubt too sugary. The drinks were even smaller – you would have had to buy three cups of tea or coffee to get enough to fill one standard mug. And, finally, the ice cream was a tiny dollop of soft stuff that even children would devour in one mouthful.

"I last saw a place like this in a Carry On film!" said Mark, laughing. "It looks like a works canteen from the 1950s".

"Yes", Emma agreed. "But at least the prices are stuck in the 1950s too!" It was incredibly cheap. In every sense of the word.

After leaving the self-titled 'department store', we all went back to the market and wandered around there for another hour or so, buying a serious ice cream from one of the stalls. But the market really was rather disappointing. And none of us could see quite why so many people visited the place if it was like this every year.

The village of Tingsryd, by contrast, set as it was just above the lake, was altogether more interesting. And when it came time to leave, we made a point of driving around a few of the roads – those which hadn't been closed for the market – to get a better feel for the place. To our surprise, even mine and Emma's, the village seemed to have as much industry as it did housing.

"There seems to be lots of work here", said Kate, as we headed back home along quiet roads. "Even back there. All those small industrial buildings".

"Yes", Emma replied. "I don't know how easy it is to find work, but there does seem to be a lot of industry. But I get the feeling that it's a country which welcomes people who want to set up a business. Even if, from what we've been told, the taxes can often be pretty tough".

*

In mid-August, the saga of the gate returned.

As a child I recalled hearing about 'Norse sagas' but only had a vague recollection of what they were about. Something to do with

197

wolves, trolls, battles and the like. Recurring themes that dragged out over many years.

Well, there were no wolves or trolls in this one. No swords. No dragons. But it was certainly a Nordic saga which began to feel as if it could drag on for years.

Emma, to her credit, had more or less forgotten about the gate and the (albeit slight) need for one. In fact, to be honest, she hadn't forgotten about it, because every now and then I brought the subject up again. But she did keep trying to find other things for me to do, to focus on, so that I would forget about the gate.

So it was that I found myself repainting a wall on one day and rehanging the cellar door on the next. But, like it or not, sooner or later, something would crop up that brought the gate back to the front of my DIY thoughts.

And in August it was, of all things, a walk along a railway line that took me back to the subject.

Taking a walk through the forest one day, along a new route I hadn't explored before, I found my path being crossed by the main railway line from Växjö to Kalmar. The railway line, at this point, was single track. And that made sense. Trains would always meet and pass at a station so there was no point struggling to build and maintain thousands of miles of double tracks in the forest. But that also gave the line a Wild West sort of feel to it. Like something made by pioneers. And as a slow goods train rumbled past, with bells clanging on a nearby level crossing, I half expected one of the wagons to be blown apart by the likes of Butch Cassidy and the Sundance Kid.

Normally, and naturally enough, I didn't walk along railway lines. There are easier ways to get yourself killed. And safer places to go for a stroll. But this was rural Sweden. The forest. Miles from anyone. And apart from being able to see any approaching trains for quite some distance, I could have heard one ten minutes before it appeared. Such was the quiet of the skog, with only flies and birds making any noise.

Besides which, walking through a Swedish forest was often anything but easy. Frequently hard going, a battle to find or make a path, and often meaning you had to give up and double back, for once it felt simpler to just walk along the iron rails. Or from sleeper to sleeper. And so that was what I did.

It was peaceful. Safe. And yes, it did feel like I had gone back in time to the 1800s and was walking along some tracks in California or Oregon.

After about half an hour or so of that, the forest receded a little, the space opened up and I found myself beside some run down railway buildings. Things which probably had been there since the 1800s. Semi derelict, with ragwort and other weeds growing all over. Rusted iron objects. Wood turned grey by the years.

As a child, with my friends, I had often played on sites like these. Old industrial sites. Derelict buildings. And they still held a fascination for me. And these railway buildings were no different. I loved the creaking the corrugated metal made in the warm wind. It was fun to surprise a sleeping cat or, as in this case, disturb a lizard resting in the sun. And there were always, always, things that could be brought back to use...

"You should see the wood out there", I told Emma later. "Planks of the stuff. Years old but still solid".

She knew where this was leading and tried to distract me by telling me about some gossip she had heard in the village shop.

It didn't work. "And railway sleepers. Dozens of them. Clearly not wanted. Not any more".

Eventually Emma gave up. "Yes, but what good is any of that to us?"

"The gate", I said. Firmly. Immediately. "We must be able to make a really good solid garden gate from that lot".

Emma nodded. "If we could get the stuff back here, and if you were any good at woodwork, maybe. But remember your previous attempt?"

She was right, of course. We had a trailer. We could easily have gone and collected a few planks of timber. The material just wasn't the problem. It was my atrocious joinery skills that were the problem.

Spotting my hesitation, Emma took her chance.

"When I was in the shop, looking at the notices, I saw a couple advertising snickeri services. You know, woodworking. Handyman. We could always ask one those..."

I knew it made sense, and making some quick excuse about being too busy 'to make my own gate anyway', I went up to the shop to get some numbers.

I collected the phone numbers of three 'snickerers' in total. And a couple of hours later, the first of them showed up.

Jens, who turned out to be Danish, was very keen and very polite. He had only recently relocated to Sweden from the northernmost part of Denmark and he was, so he said, still acclimatising to a world full of trees and no horizon, having come from a place with nothing but horizon and no trees.

I liked Jens and Emma seemed to like him too. We even invited him for a cup of coffee as we discussed my ideas for the gate.

But, sadly, that was where the problems began. I soon saw that his calculations, the material he was going to use, his design, all of it, was more in keeping with an entrance to a stately home or chateau rather than our drive.

Our home was big. The drive was pretty long. But we just wanted a garden gate. Jens was plotting a drawbridge, gatehouse and watch tower by the looks of things.

I had never met many Danes before. If any. And I wondered, as we waved goodbye, whether they were all so inclined to go off topic and make grandiose schemes. Maybe that was why their country – which was essentially a lot of islands – was linked together by a set of spectacular bridges. Probably the original plans had only been for some simple wooden structures.

The second number on my list never replied. I rang it several times but the ringing tone sounded wrong. I tried to leave a message but just kept getting beeping noises.

I tried again a few days later. Still nothing. How could it be so bloody hard to get a garden gate?

So I turned to the third number. Rang it, and got an answer.

Yes, Olof (a different Olof from our chatty plumber who organised the charity calendars) would be happy to look at the job.

When could he call round? The next day, about midday.

Sure enough, as punctual as everything and everyone seemed to be in Sweden, the following day, at exactly noon, a car began bumping along our drive.

"Oh my goodness", said Emma, watching it from the window, "Look at the condition of this old banger!"

I watched as a very old Volvo – not a classic, just a worn out old model from the 1980s – spluttered and staggered along our drive.

"Whoever chose that shade of orange?" I asked, more of myself than of Emma.

The car rolled to a stop, and for a moment I'm sure both of us wondered if it would ever move again or remain there, broken down, blocking our drive. But then the door opened – slowly, very slowly – and a very old man got out of the car, also very slowly.

It didn't look too promising.

"He looks like an undertaker from a western!" laughed Emma.

And it was true. Olof did have that sort of air about him. But, then, looking on the positive side, if he *was* an undertaker, at least that would mean he was pretty handy with wood.

We both went out to meet 'the undertaker' rather than ask or expect him to climb up the stairs to the front door. I think both of us were worried that if he climbed up, rather like his old orange Volvo, he might never move again. He looked older and older the closer we got.

"Haloo", he said as we approached.

In truth, perhaps needless to say, Olof the Undertaker was actually a very nice man. Softly spoken, with icily clear blue eyes and hands that had, quite clearly, spent a lifetime doing manual work.

The three of us walked along the drive together, and he told us about the mill which used to stand here – where our house now stood.

"Of course, that was over two hundred years ago", he finished.

Emma caught my eye, and I suspect we were both wondering the same thing. But no, surely, even this ancient chap wasn't quite *that* old.

Our discussion about the gate was brief. I told him I wanted something wooden. Heavy. Three or five bars. He said five would look better. Quite stylish. I agreed with that. And, of course, I also said, waterproof. Yes, that too, he agreed. Painted or oiled? Whichever he thought best.

And that was it.

A man who resembled Father Time was going to make my gate. And it wouldn't take very long and it wouldn't cost very much. The equivalent of a few hundred pounds sterling.

Why hadn't I thought of asking a 'snickerer' sooner?

Emma and I waved him off and watched – with some trepidation – as he started up the old car, and with even more concern as a great cloud of smoke blew out of the exhaust. But, finally, it moved, and eventually disappeared, very slowly, around the bend in the road.

"I hope his car lasts long enough for him to deliver the gate", said Emma as we turned back to the house.

I thought the same about Olof himself, but didn't say as much.

*

The end of August had arrived, and it felt rather sad. It wasn't that either Emma or I disliked autumn; it was more that Sweden in summer was fun. Very outdoorsy. Much more so than anything we had experienced before.

Of course that made good sense. With a short autumn, a very long winter, and a short spring, and being such a beautiful country, it made sense to get out and about as much as possible in the summer, with all those extra hours of sunlight.

"Let's have one last trip out before September arrives", I suggested.

Emma agreed willingly. She had been working flat out on the computer for the last week and both wanted and needed to get some fresh air.

"Actually", she said, "I have just the thing..."

And after a quick rummage in her office drawer, she produced a leaflet.

"What's that?" I asked.

"A trail. A bicycle trail. Apparently there are loads of these in Sweden. It's a huge pastime here."

I took the leaflet and glanced through it.

It was a cycle trail, which followed a part of the so-called 'Emigrant Trail'.

The leaflet, in full colour, contained a detailed map of the route, with a list of numbered points and sights to look out for along the way.

"Looks good", I said. "Yeah. Why not? Let's do that. It'd be a lovely way to finish the summer".

We had bicycles and used them occasionally. But we both wanted to use them more often. And if Sweden really did have a number of these routes, it made sense to start discovering them.

We planned to go the following day: the very last day of August.

Needless to say, I checked on the weather. But the forecast was ideal. Warm and dry, but not too hot.

Emma popped up to the village shop and bought a few supplies for the day. And we went to bed looking forward to it immensely.

From the 1840s onwards, for the best part of 60 or so years, hundreds of thousands of Swedes left Sweden and migrated to the United States, mainly settling in Mid-West states like Montana. In total, almost a sixth of the population moved to the USA during that time – a staggering figure.

Particularly affected was the central Småland region – which matches up pretty well with the modern day county of Kronoberg. This was because land in that region was particularly tough for growing crops, though there were political and social reasons for the mass upheaval too.

Emma and I had frequently seen signs referring to the 'trail' the emigrants had taken, out of Småland, with their few belongings, as they headed for the coast and ships to take them to America and a new life.

And although we hadn't really looked into the history of it all, strangely, we felt a little like kindred spirits as we in turn had left our own homeland to move to Sweden.

Today, that 'trail' is a more or less clearly defined route, with facilities along the way for hikers, tourists and – of course – cyclists.

"So", I said as we drove along the next day, with our bicycles fixed to the roof rack. "Where do we start? What do we see first?"

Emma was checking the map and the leaflet to make sure we parked in the right place and didn't get lost.

"Well, we'll just do a short stint today", she replied. "The whole route is 130 km and I think that, after not having ridden for ages, just 10 km or 20 km will do us".

I agreed. "And we mustn't forget that however far we go in one direction, we have to turn around and come back. I don't suppose the immigrants took a circular route!"

We found a place to park. There was no one at all around. The parking was free. And we unloaded the bikes and set off at a leisurely pace, trying to follow the route.

It wasn't easy. Not least because I don't think we were in the right place. But the countryside was very pretty all the same, and we cycled along enjoying the peace and quiet.

"Where are we?" I finally asked Emma.

"I'm not sure" she replied, turning the leaflet around as she looked at it. "I think we're near a village called Skruv. And there are supposed to be several things of interest to see just here".

We both looked up. There was forest. And not very much else.

"It says there's a hill near here, covered with juniper bushes".

I looked around. There might well have been a hill nearby. Or even several hills. It didn't seem like something to draw our attention to.

"What else?"

Emma frowned as she read the leaflet. "Old fashioned wooden houses."

We couldn't see any from where we had stopped. But it would hardly have been a surprise if we had been able to see 'old fashioned wooden houses'. The country was littered with the things.

We cycled slowly along a little more. It was a beautiful and gentle ride. But neither of us felt that we were really getting any kind of a feel for the immigrants or their trail.

"I half expect the leaflet to say something like 'on your left there is an old farmhouse'. It all seems so... ordinary", said Emma as we rode along.

"A little further on, you can see lots of trees!" I laughed. And pedalled a bit faster.

"And in the next field you will find a large stone. Next to which is another large stone!" Emma shouted after me.

But the thing is, that *was* Sweden. That was what it was like. Rural Sweden at any rate. In terms of producing a tourist leaflet, there just wasn't all that much to write about. Of course, the fact that so many people had had to uproot themselves and cross half the world was a hugely moving story. But there was no real evidence of that story. Nothing left to see other than a hill or a church, an old barn or a crossroads. And that was just so typically Swedish.

September

The children had all gone back to school in mid-August. Numerous holiday attractions had closed then, too, and the ice cream boat, at Karlshamn was now only open at the weekend. For most Swedes, the next proper break would be Christmas.

Emma and I, both working from home, had never had that long summer lay-off. But, then, nor did we have to 'return' to work in mid-August. And so if the sun shone, on any day of the week, we could take the laptops outside and work in the warmth.

The same also applied to the beach. If it was sunny, if the day looked good enough, we could go down for an afternoon – with or without our work – and spend a few hours by the sea. And one day, in very early September, with the sun shining in a clear blue sky, that was what we decided to do.

There was plenty of warmth in the day, a quick glance at my thermometers told me that, at noon, it was already 24 °C. And it felt even milder than that.

"Shall I put our swimming stuff in the boot?" Emma asked. We had taken it out a week earlier, assuming that summer was over.

I looked up once more at the sky. "Yes. Why not?"

People are basically the same wherever you go. But from culture to culture and country to country, there are always slight differences. Some of those differences seem somehow better: a good idea. Some of them seem worse. It's mostly just a question of personal preferences. We had thoroughly enjoyed living in Sweden so far, and that, in no small measure, was down to the friendly and welcoming nature of the Swedes themselves. They looked after their country and their countryside, and they respected both nature and one another. Yet, at the same time, in terms of technology and in areas of society, the country was very modern. And ready to change and embrace change. But there were also areas where we felt things still needed to be improved. And that was the case with every country. Every person. Everything. We were none of us perfect. And one of those things in Sweden, clearly, was food. Organic food was becoming more widespread, but the variety and quality of food – in general – was poor.

And as we drove down wide roads even emptier than usual, with the sun high overhead, another area we thought we could see room for manoeuvre was in terms of summer.

As we pulled up at the car park just behind our favourite beach in Karlshamn, and saw that ours was the only vehicle there we agreed how strange it was that the Swedes packed up in mid-August when the weather could still be this good in September.

We knew that, back in the UK, some holiday destinations like Torquay would still be very busy – crowded almost – right through until half-term in October. Over the years, the British had extended their holiday season – and rightly so. It works better for the resorts, as the season is extended. It works better for the tourists too, because they can choose to go on holiday at a cheaper time of year. And if the weather isn't always quite as good, there are always other things to be enjoyed. In any case, as a child, I remembered plenty of cold, grey and wet days even in July.

On this particular day, rather than go straight down onto the beach, we first climbed up onto the rocks overlooking the little bay. It was a bit of a scramble to climb up, but more than worth the effort. The view was wonderful. The water of the bay, stretched out beneath us, was crystal clear again – a beautiful turquoise over a sandy bottom, with a few small rafts of seaweed and a few submerged rocks visible. Back in the summer we had swum over those and dived down to them to discover the small fish and other animals which used the rocks for shelter.

Down on the beach, however, there was no one about. The small wooden cabins where people got changed during the summer appeared to be closed for the winter.

It didn't matter. This was Sweden. There was no one around. In a little while we would get changed and go for a dip. But first, we sat, relaxed, ate a few sandwiches and just felt glad to be alive and happy to be in Sweden.

And for an hour, that was all we did.

Then a small council van of some kind arrived and parked in the car park. Three men got out of it wearing fluorescent vests and carrying an assortment of tools – mostly things like brooms and shovels. We watched them as they walked down to the beach, and began working beside the wooden cabins, clearing something away and marking the ground with chalk, talking all the while.

Of course five minutes later the beautiful peaceful afternoon was interrupted. The Swedes were all back at work. And that included these men. And from their van they had now extricated a pneumatic drill, and where they had marked the ground with chalk, the drill was now busily – and noisily – at work.

"Oh dammit", said Emma, who had already got changed into her swimming costume.

I looked at her. Looked at the men. Listened to the noise. Then glanced at the sea.

"Never mind", I said. "We've had a nice couple of hours. Let's have a quick swim anyway. After all, this might be the last nice day for a week or so".

Emma agreed. I got changed too, and we scrambled down from the rocks and went out onto the beach.

We didn't notice at first, but the three men had stopped drilling to watch us.

Because we were about to discover just why Sweden and the Swedes all go back to work in mid-August.

The water, the sea, the Baltic, may have been invitingly blue. Crystal clear. All of that. But it was also totally, shockingly, absolutely bloody freezing.

I'm glad to say that Emma screamed the loudest.

But I screamed too. Because it really was that cold.

Clearly, at some point after mid-August, the nights in Sweden must turn pretty cold. And with their arrival, the warmer sea temperatures pack their bags and head south.

At first both of us retreated back out of the water.

But that, of course, would never do.

There were Swedish workmen watching.

We couldn't let the side down.

In any case the sun was warm. The day was warm. Once back on the beach and dried off, we would be fine. So there was only one thing to do. We held hands and ran. Straight back into the ice-cold water of the bay.

I have to say that for around 20 minutes or so, it *was* fun. A lot of fun. Refreshing. Bitingly cold or not. Maybe because it was such a warm day, or maybe because those workmen were there, we enjoyed it. There was something shockingly Scandinavian about being in the sea on that day, but also, at the same time, something very British.

Eventually, however, the cold began to take its toll. And we'd had enough. Besides, the workmen had gone back to work. We had 'won'.

And next year? We laughed about that. Probably our swimming costumes could be safely put away in August. Just like they were in the rest of Sweden.

*

Just a few days after our brave but cold dip in the Baltic, the weather changed very much for the worse. September may have begun with summer-like temperatures, but it clearly wasn't going to continue in that fashion. This was Sweden after all.

There was a jogging circuit in the woods of the nearest small town, and Emma and I had gone round it once or twice in the summer. Newly laid and floodlit, it allowed you to walk through the forest without it being a struggle. It had been a warm walk in the summer, pleasant and green. But by the end of the first week in September, it had a frosty feel to it reminiscent of twilight much later in the year.

"Well, it's definitely autumn now", said Emma, as we walked along the path again one evening.

There was a smell of damp leaves in the air, and of dry soil slowly being turned to a thin mud.

The next day the sun was out. But the air was much cooler than it had been only recently. The thinner leaved trees – things like birch and alder – were already turning bright yellow and dark orange. And although such autumnal colours were beginning to shine and looked glorious, it was another reminder that we were in a very northern climate.

Yet another came that same evening.

Whoever had owned our house before, they, or maybe their grandparents, had planted a wonderful selection of apple trees. Some of these had borne fruit as early as mid-August. Lightly flavoured apples with a pale skin. Old varieties, we were sure. Full of flavour. But now, and quite suddenly, we had an abundance of fruit, as several large trees all reached their peak at the same moment.

I had already begun collecting as many of these apples as I could easily reach, and had even started to store them carefully in the cellar, each individually wrapped, in a collection of old wooden drawers which we had bought cheaply from a charity shop.

But there were still plenty of them on the trees. And it would take a stepladder to reach them.

A stepladder. Or a long neck.

And the long neck got there before I did.

Autumn was coming, if not already here, and winter was certainly coming too. And the wild animals knew that better than we did. Any chance of a free meal was too good an opportunity to miss.

Emma and I watched the moose as they emerged from the forest, a troupe of half a dozen or so, at first timidly and then with more certainty – and we couldn't bring ourselves to go outside and shoo them off. Our apples may have been a little out of my reach, but for the giant moose, stretching both long necks and long legs, they were a handy snack.

"Will they get drunk on them?" Emma asked as we watched in the fast fading light.

I shrugged. I had no idea. But even if they did, who could blame them? Winter would be long and hard for us. And we had central heating and a car to take us to the shops. If I'd been living out there in the wild, I would have wanted to get drunk too.

Funnily enough, the chance to do just that arrived the very next day via a phone call from an old friend who we hadn't seen for years.

Paul, who I'd known since childhood, was a real character. I had first met him many years earlier, sitting crying in a telephone box. We were both only 12 years old at the time, but I'd never forgotten it. And after initially telling me to just go away, he revealed that he was being bullied by a couple of other boys. I told him to come out of the phone box and that I would help him. I did. I gave both of those other boys black eyes. And from then on we became firm friends.

Two years later, he had come out as gay. That was at the end of the 1970s at a time where being gay was still wholly frowned upon and not at all easy to do. And at the time, he had only been 14 years old.

At 15 he had left home, and left school, just as soon he was legally allowed. From there he had lived one adventure after another, crossing my path only once every few years. But we had remained friends. And he had met Emma and the two of them had gotten on very well.

The last time we had actually seen him, he was setting off to San Francisco to live with his new partner. Following that move, for a short while we had lost touch. But then with the advent of Facebook and Twitter, he had once more come back into our lives.

"You're not going to believe this, but I'm in Sweden and, of all places, I am here in Växjo. Now. Tonight. Just for one night. Right now." Following a long helllooo, these were the first words he said. "So, tell me, where are you exactly? I can come and pick you up. It can't be far. And don't tell me you're too busy. Come on, get your best boots on. Let's go out for a drink."

It turned out that Paul was working on some contract or other in Germany and, as part of that, along with two colleagues, he had flown into Växjö airport earlier that very day to have a business meeting. There would be another one in the morning, before a flight back to Dusseldorf, so that left him free for one whole evening and already feeling bored. "I've got one whole night in Sweden and I'm not going to spend it sitting in a hotel bar trying to chat up a good looking young waiter. Hmm... Although maybe on second thoughts!" he laughed.

As soon as I could get a word in edgeways, I explained where we were.

"But you're not too busy to come out?" he asked. And as he did so, I recalled that small boy in the phone box all those years ago.

"No. No! We'd love to. It would be wonderful to see you again!" I said. And I meant it. It had been a few weeks since our last visitors left and a night out was long overdue. In any case, Paul meant a lot to me.

Even better, Emma volunteered to drive, and that suited me just fine. Because it meant that I could have a drink.

Often, Paul was an ebullient character. Sometimes that could border on the rude. He would say what others felt, but didn't dare say – or would have been too embarrassed to say. It wasn't that he meant any harm, he just had a quick wit, and liked to laugh and make others laugh. And neither Emma nor I could wait to see what he would make of Sweden, its bars, restaurants, the people...

It was a dry and mildish evening. So we arrived in Växjö, parked the car near the main railway station, and decided to walk around to the hotel where Paul had promised to wait for us.

He was outside, smoking a cigarette. We knew it was him from two hundred metres away. In part because of the way he walked – he paced up and down with the cigarette like a man waiting outside a maternity ward. But in part because of the way he dressed.

"Is he wearing a skirt?" asked Emma as we got closer.

We walked up to him, and he flicked the cigarette through the air, a huge smile crossed his face and we had a three way hug.

"What *have* you got on?" Emma asked with a smile.

"A kilt. It's a kilt, not a skirt. Oh, I know. It's plain black. But isn't it gorgeous? Canvas. Not wool..."

Close up or even from a distance, Paul could have passed for a Swede. He had blond hair (dyed since childhood), fine cheekbones, and had always kept himself slim and in good shape.

For the next 20 minutes or so, neither Emma nor I could get a word out. Paul told us about his work, the hotel, giving up smoking, not giving up smoking, his latest partner, the flight to

Sweden, what he had been doing recently, where he planned to go next and then, finally, he asked "So, where shall we go first? A drink. Then a bite to eat!"

He always asked and answered his own questions. He was the only person who could keep up with himself.

There is a chain of pubs in Sweden called The Bishop's Arms. And so that was where we went first. Emma and I had looked these up before our move to Sweden. We hadn't minded the change of country, the longer winters, and so forth, but we didn't want to live in a country without a pub.

"Oh my gawwd", said Paul expansively as we entered the pub, heads already turning to look. "This is sooo like a pub my Dad used to take me into. In the 1970s!"

There was dark wood, beermats on the bar, brass fittings, dark red seats. It was very much like an English pub from 30 or more years ago. But we liked it anyway.

"What will you have?" I asked, as Emma and Paul took a table for the three of us.

"Mmmm... I'll have one of those, please", Paul replied, raising his eyebrows at one of the male bar staff.

"Behave", laughed Emma.

The night continued in much the same vein from there.

For my own part, I drank three pints of cider, and a double whisky far too quickly. I was no longer used to it and my head was already beginning to swirl as we all left the pub to visit a nearby restaurant. So from there on I decided I wouldn't drink any more alcohol. But Paul had other ideas.

Even though quite slightly built, he had spent many years going to night clubs and bars and was used to drinking. "I'm going to celebrate with a good bottle of wine", he said as looked at the drinks menu.

"It'll be expensive", Emma warned him.

"I don't care", Paul laughed. "Let's get two bottles. It's all on expenses this evening!"

The wine arrived before – long before – the food. We had warned Paul that Swedish food wasn't necessarily all that one might desire. And so the delay prompted him to stop the waiter and ask "Is there a problem with the microwave?"

Fortunately the waiter didn't quite understand what Paul was driving at. Besides, both of them seemed more interested in each other than they did in the food.

Växjö had seemed so tame, so ordinary when we had visited it alone. But now, it was beginning to feel like Berlin in the 1930s. Or maybe that was just because Paul was showing the waiter his 'skirt'. Some people at another table were interested in it too.

"It *is* a kilt!" he insisted again, as Emma felt the material.

By the time the food finally did arrive I had drunk too much of Paul's wine and had no real idea if it was any good or not. Sadly, as Emma assured me afterwards, it was actually pretty decent.

The restaurant too was very pleasant. Very stylish. Not too warm. Tables well spaced out. Polite conversation going on in the background. Subtle lighting. Once more – as we had seen before – Swedes knew how to create the right ambiance.

Paul got the bill for us. And he disappeared up to the bar to pay it.

"Where has he got to?" Emma asked after ten minutes had passed.

Finally Paul came back. "All done", he smiled. "And I even got this". He held up a scrap of paper. Emma took a look at it and laughed. It was the name and phone number of the waiter.

"Paul", she said. "We can't take you anywhere!"

"I didn't ask him", replied Paul, feigning indignation. "He offered it to me! You never know, I might have to make a few more trips to Sweden yet!"

*

We had almost forgotten Olof, old Olof, the genial 'undertaker'-turned-gate maker. But the end of September saw another visit from Old Father Time. Not once had we called him or pressed him to bring us the gate, but – like all Swedes we had met so far – he was as good as his word.

I had just come out of the cellar when a somehow familiar spluttering noise caught my attention. I looked up and saw the old orange Volvo. Still going, and still struggling to make it along our drive.

Half way along it came to a stop, and out climbed Olof, wearing a denim bib and braces.

I had no idea how old he actually was, but I was certain that if I could be as sprightly by the time I was the same age, I would be very happy.

I walked up to drive towards him. We met, we shook hands. He half looked up at the sky and said, without any hesitation, "It will snow at Christmas this year".

Overhead was pale blue and cloudless. Cool. But pleasant. And still as dry as dry could be.

"How do you know that?" I asked him.

Those crystal clear blue eyes fixed mine for a moment. "Every winter, since even my childhood, if the cranes flew south before my father's birthday, then it would snow at Christmas".

For a moment I wondered if his father was still alive. But I didn't dare ask.

"And did they fly south early this year then?" I asked.

"Very long time before. So there will be a lot of snow this winter. And at Christmas".

I had no reason to doubt him but I made a mental note to check if he was right. And – if he was – to keep an eye on migrating cranes in future years.

"So", said Olof, cutting into my thoughts, "Your gate. I have it here in the boot of my car".

He took the gate out of his car easily. Although it was in two parts, he still achieved that a bit too easily for my liking. I was hoping it was going to be a pretty heavy thing. But no, instead it was fairly lightweight. All the same, it was a very lovely piece of work. And I had no right or need to complain. He had even carved some of the bars with a sort of fretwork.

So much in Sweden was made of wood that it really seemed quite natural to me they would be able to produce handicrafts of this quality. This was traditional work. Skills that went back centuries.

"Oh Emma must come and see this", I said.

But she had already spotted Olof and I talking and was coming up the drive to see the new gate.

"Here you are", I said, as if I had made it myself (and conveniently forgetting my own awful efforts earlier in the year). "I knew we would be able to get a nice gate. Handmade too."

"Oh, it's lovely", said Emma.

Olof looked like he was going to blush. But he didn't.

We stood and admired it for a few minutes, and then Emma insisted Olof come into the house for a cup of coffee and some cake. (We had learned, by now, that coffee and cake was the normal thing to do. Forget about alcohol, cigarettes or savoury snacks).

We had been sitting there for about 30 minutes and Olof was already on his third slice of cake when somehow, the subject of the Vasa, the famous Swedish galleon came up. The Vasa was a bit like the Mary Rose in that it was a famous wooden warship which sank on its maiden voyage and had – centuries later – been discovered and brought back to the surface where it was now preserved as the centrepiece of a museum in Stockholm.

Emma had long wanted to go and see it.

So she asked Olof if he had ever been to the museum, assuming, naturally enough, that he would have been very interested in the craftsmanship involved in creating such a magnificent vessel.

"Oh no", said Olof, "No. Indeed I have never been to Stockholm".

We were both surprised to hear this. And even more surprised when he went on to tell us that he had never been to Gothenburg either nor even the much closer Malmo.

"Never?" asked Emma incredulously.

Olof shook his head. "I don't go often even to Växjö. There are too many people. And too many shops".

It turned out that he had been to Kalmar – once – as part of his compulsory military service. But, other than that, this was very much a man of Kronoberg who had spent his entire life here, surrounded by trees, wild animals and good healthy clean air.

And it showed.

A short while after the old orange Volvo had puffed and wheezed its way off our drive, I realised that I had made a mistake with the gate.

"There aren't any gate posts", I told Emma.

"Did you ask him to make you any gate posts?"

I shook my head. "No. It's my mistake not his. I just never gave them a thought until now".

For a few minutes I considered giving Olof a call and asking him to pop back. But then, remembering the wood I had found on the railway line, railway sleepers, planks, all sorts, I decided that I could knock up a few gate posts myself. One way or the other. After all, I said to myself, how hard could it be?

Two days later, I found out just how hard it could be.

I still didn't have any gate posts, but I had worked out where I wanted to put the gate. I had marked out two points for making holes into which gates posts would fit, and then it was time to try to make the holes.

Digging a few holes, even holes deep enough for gate posts, oughtn't to take an able bodied man more than an hour or two. At least, that was the case everywhere else in Europe. Sweden was a different matter altogether.

First to go was my trusty old garden fork, which I had used for 20 years. Naturally enough, I began digging with that. But the shaft split and gave way before the tough Swedish ground did.

No matter, I said to myself. I needed a new fork anyway. I have a pick axe. That will make light work of the job.

And so I trudged back to the cellar and collected the pick axe. Emma called to me and asked if I wanted dinner. I shouted back that I would have some in ten minutes or so, just as soon as I had finished making the holes.

But I was wrong again. The pick suffered almost the same fate as the garden fork. The head began to wobble long before any kind of hole began to appear.

Clearly the Kronoberg ground was a tough old bird. It was more like concrete than soil.

For a little while, now getting frustrated, I dug manually, finally pulling out one small lump of granite and imagining that had been the issue.

I tried the pick axe again.

Same problem.

Emma came out and asked me if I was going to be long.

"There must be loads of stones in there", I muttered.

She agreed, and went back inside.

Never mind. I also had a sledge hammer, a large crow bar and an assortment of cold chisels.

I went back to the cellar, gathered a handful of tools, and dragged myself along the 200 metre long drive again.

But no. Still the same result.

Even smashing chisels into the 'dirt', and levering at them, sweating and cursing, after another 30 minutes or so I had barely dug a hole big enough to bury a goldfish in a matchbox.

What the hell is Sweden made of? I wondered.

Briefly, I thought about bringing my drill out, on an extra-long extension lead, but then Emma called me once more. It really was time to eat.

I looked up at the sky. By now it was cold and almost dark.

I sighed.

"Sod it", I said out loud. I would come back to it tomorrow.

Or the day after.

I leaned the new gate against a tree trunk, rounded up all the tools and went inside to have a shower, some supper and an early night. I was exhausted.

"Bloody gate", I muttered.

October

As October came around, Emma and I noticed once more just how impossible it was to ignore the weather in Sweden. We had lived in the UK and complained about the rain and the lack of summer along with 50 million other people. But it – the weather – had never meant any more to us than that. It was just something to moan about while waiting in a queue to buy a packet of chips.

Sweden was *very* different. Month after month the weather and its extremes of sun, cold, snow or dry were important features of our day-to-day life. They were no longer things in the background, in the way they were if you lived in a big city; they were things that directly affected what you could do and when you could do it. They were things you had to check up on almost every day. In much the same way, we had friends in France who talked, all the time, about the food there. France, it seemed, was mostly about food. Sweden was mostly about weather.

So it was that for the first week of October things were still quite mild. But this, combined with the slow loss of leaves and moisture in the air, created a fog the likes of which we had only previously seen in films about Jack the Ripper.

Day after day the fog hung in the air. Clinging, almost dangling and swinging, from the branches of the trees. Sitting just above the surface of the road and hiding every passing vehicle until the very last moment.

It was otherworldly.

Somewhere up there was sunshine and a blue sky. But it wasn't showing itself down here at ground level.

Now and then a brief – very brief – glimpse of brighter light would cut through the gloom and a blaze of orange or bright yellow leaves would reveal the world of autumn to our eyes which otherwise were slowly being accustomed to only seeing in the dark.

But even those short bursts of sun would soon pass and then the fog would seal back up and cut us off once more to leave us quite alone in the forest. Well, alone with the barking deer, bellowing moose and who knew what else.

The forest itself felt somehow heavier than it had been, too. In winter, under the snow, it had been a duvet. Thick, white and apparently lifeless. In summer it had all turned green. And it had felt light, ethereal almost. Indeed if it hadn't been for the mosquitos and other assorted biting insects, I would have slept out in the forest during the summer. It drew a person in; it was enticing, almost cheerful. But now? Under the October fog? No.

It had become heavy. And that was the only word for it. Dripping like a soaked cloth and matting itself leaf by leaf to the ground.

Despite the clinging damp, however, we went for a few long walks in the skog and, in its own way, it was still quite fascinating and well worth the effort. For a start, once away from the road, the silence was really quite eerie. Crows – or something like them, it was hard to say what they were in the fog – took off from tree tops as we walked past, black shadowy shapes lifting off into the grey and then disappearing from view. We felt as if we were walking through a Bergman film set.

At ground level, the usual narrow twisting footpaths were now narrow twisting lines of mud created by feet of all kinds. None of which, apart from ours, were human. We studied the footprints carefully and even took a notepad on one walk to sketch the different types so that we could look them up on the internet once we got back home.

Some were easy enough to recognise. Deer, boar, fox and moose. Some were harder to place, but we decided they were hare and even little weasel trails. Other, bigger footprints, were not to be found on the internet. And we eventually wondered if, out there, in all that untouched deep dark forest, there were actually things that no one really knew about.

A big part of Swedish folklore concerns the troll. And after one particularly foggy and dark walk, we were sure that we had seen some. Great dark cloaked figures that froze as you looked at them only to disappear as you approached. Or perhaps it was just tricks of that strangely dim light. We couldn't be sure.

Also on the ground, along with the footprints, there were a plethora of mushrooms of all sizes and colours. Some as big as a football, off white and quite alien looking. Others were bright red with white spots – the classic toadstool.

Edvard told us that many of these mushrooms were edible but that we oughtn't to pick them unless we did so with a guide. So, on one slightly brighter weekend afternoon, we did just that. We went out for a walk in the skog with Jack the Canadian who said he knew what was what in terms of mushrooms and promised us a tasty treat or two.

At first that walk followed a trail that Emma and I knew quite well. Then Jack took us off into a bit of forest so dark that for all the world it might as well have been night time. We had little battery powered head torches and we definitely needed them to see our way.

That particular dark walk lasted for about 20 minutes and we emerged to find ourselves in a small grassy area.

Grass, we realised, was now a rare sight for us.

We saw lawns, of course, and our own untidy patch of ill-kempt green stuff. But once away from houses, the world consisted of trees, rocks, water and lots more trees. Grass was really nowhere to be seen, and even where a clearing had been made for sheep or cattle, the grass was a poor scrubby affair and ought, really, to have been called something other than grass. It wasn't green. It wasn't soft. And from what we could see, a good number of the livestock didn't rate it as particularly edible either.

Jack then proceeded to show us around this greenish clearing for a little while and picked a selection of some of the strangest looking fungi we had ever seen. Little yellow trumpets, which to our eyes looked positively toxic, were, he assured us, the extremely tasty chanterelle mushroom. Once we saw them close up we could see that. But in the wild they looked scarier and not to be trusted. He also cut a chunk out of one of the big white footballs and told us that we should take it home and fry it in butter. It was the size of a decent steak.

Finally he showed us a pair of innocent looking white mushrooms. Not particularly monstrous and quite definitely the sort of thing that an amateur might fancy taking home for the frying pan. In fact these were mushrooms called 'Destroying Angels', and despite their innocent appearance they were highly poisonous.

Mushroom picking wasn't the only typically autumnal pastime that kept me busy outdoors.

Back in the spring, with the ground outside so hard that a garden fork couldn't be pushed into it, I had decided to grow as much fruit and as many vegetables as possible using a deep bed system.

I had used such a system once before in the UK and it had been very productive. Much more so than growing vegetables direct in the soil. And it had seemed to make sense to patiently wait out the last few weeks of winter by creating some more of these beds.

I soon had the whole thing pretty well organised. I'd needed bags of peat, bags of manure, some timber and a few nails and stakes. And, once begun, it wasn't too hard a job to construct them. At first I'd planned to make about a half dozen deep beds. But winter didn't finish on cue, so I ended up making 18 of the things.

Our neighbour Edvard had never seen a deep bed before, and he was initially dubious, especially as I had built so many of them. But that had just made me all the more determined to grow a lot more than I'd ever done before. After all, if there is one thing Britain can produce it's a good gardener. And that was going to be me!

Sure enough, by midsummer, not only was Edvard wholly convinced of my gardening prowess but, from time to time, passers-by from the village stopped and stared in amazement. I even saw someone taking a photo with their phone.

And no wonder.

Now and then a house in the village would have a few lettuce in a sickly looking row surrounded by lawn. Or maybe a few carrots or cabbages. But my garden – at least the vegetable element of it – looked like a full-blown professional nursery. I had 18 beds full of everything from sweet corn to sunflowers, and the latter were fully 3 metres high.

But that was back then. In June, July and August.

Now it was mid-October.

And the wealth of produce from my vegetable garden was clearly coming to an end. Many of the beds were now empty for the winter, with stuff like turnips and courgettes long since finished.

All the same I still had large numbers of things like parsnips in the ground.

Back in the mild climate of the UK, like most people who kept an allotment, I had grown things like cabbages and parsnips right through the winter. But here in Sweden, as the fog finally gave way to clear and very cold crisp days and evenings, it was obvious to me that none of my vegetables were going to survive a Swedish winter outdoors, as even hardy plants such as sprouts and kale were starting to turn a very sickly yellow and brown around the edges.

Clearly I needed to find a way of storing them through the winter.

Fortunately the Swedes had the (almost perfect) answer.

Centuries of having to choose between starvation in winter or finding a way of storing surplus fruit and vegetables had left behind the *jordkällare* (literally 'earth cellar' and pronounced 'yordkeller'). These little buildings, often resembling a stone igloo, were to be seen everywhere, because the earth cellar was once the only way of keeping things like potatoes or carrots through the long months of cold weather.

Being sunk partly into the ground, the thick stone walls and soil kept the worst of the frost at bay, and the natural moisture keep the vegetables reasonably fresh.

Sadly, these days, although these little buildings were still quite common, the vast majority of them were now in a very tumbledown condition. Modern shops and freezers had taken away the need to store your own produce.

We were lucky, however. We had one such stone igloo in a corner of our garden, and although it needed some repair it was more or less ready to be brought back into use. Even the thick little wooden door that gave access to the cellar was still useable with just a small amount of patching up and a drop of oil on the hinges.

And so after a few days' work – plus some new pine shelf units bought from IKEA specially for the purpose – I soon had a reasonable store of swedes, leeks, carrots and so forth stacked safely in a very traditional manner.

Not wanting to put all my apples (or parsnips) in one basket, however, I also bought some sharp sand and stored some other vegetables in a wooden chest in the cellar of the house. Just in case. This was a slightly less mediaeval manner of keeping fruit and vegetables, but it was something I had done before and which I knew worked reasonably well. I also thought it would be interesting to see which method worked best.

The problem was that although I had stuffed vegetables into the earth cellar, and put others into wooden chests – and even heeled leeks into the flower bed right beside the house, on the basis that it would remain a little milder there for a few weeks longer – I still had a surplus in the ground.

The kale and sprouts in particular couldn't be stored. Not really. So, taking a quick trip to the garden centre, I bought some fleece and covered the last two deep beds with it, protecting my remaining few green vegetables from the worst of the cold. For a month or so more, Sweden could do its worst.

Or so I thought.

The very next day, after breakfast, I went out to the vegetable beds, just to check.

And to my disappointment I found the fleece to be all awry. There hadn't been any wind overnight, so my first thought was vandalism. Someone from the village had obviously been envious of my green fingers.

A closer inspection, however, showed me that I had jumped too quickly to the wrong conclusion. Because not only was the fleece all over the place, but the kale had gone. Eaten. And most of the sprouts had gone too. And all around, in the ground, on the paths, and even in places in the deep beds themselves, was tell-tale evidence of deer.

I hadn't even given them a thought.

But now it was obvious.

As winter drew slowly in, food became harder to find in the forest.

And the deer had trooped in, during the night, and had a good feed at my expense.

I had failed to safely store the last of my winter vegetables.

But I didn't care. Not a jot. I looked up at the skog and smiled. It was give and take in Sweden. Throughout the year we had eaten berries and mushrooms from the forest, and in return, the forest had eaten the last of my winter greens.

*

The fog of early October and the cold of mid-October made us realise that, however bright and warm and dry the summer had been, winter would be arriving earlier in Sweden than we might otherwise have wanted. Far from lasting the three or four months we'd been accustomed to in the UK, winter up here was more like seven months long.

Briefly, the prospect of bonus months of winter got me down. And Emma suggested – in the politest possible terms – that I go and find something to do to cheer myself up. But what?

At first I thought once more about the garden.

One of the joys of growing your own fruit and vegetables is ordering the seeds. Poring over the seed catalogues and deciding what you're going to grow and how much. It was something I looked forward to and something I enjoyed doing every autumn. But, really, this year, the prospect of next spring felt far too distant to worry about seeds and plants. The same was true about our trees. Pruning and tidying was time consuming and it gave us firewood. And we had over 100 trees, all told, which needed maintenance. But I had already done much of that work in the summer, resulting in a fine looking pile of wood, tidily stacked and drying under tarpaulin, for the following winter.

I also enjoyed the odd spot of DIY. But that wasn't going to fill very much of my time, because apart from a bit of painting to be done in the cellar, and fitting a new parquet floor in the 'studio' or guest cottage, there just wasn't that much that needed to be done.

There was also paid work, of course. Things had improved hugely in that respect for both of us as the year had worn on. We were both fortunate enough to be able to work from home using computers (which, of course, in part had enabled us to move to Sweden – even if it had been a bit of a gamble to lose contacts and so forth for a while as we moved and settled in) and that took up some hours each day.

But I was bored and needed something else to do. An excuse to get out of the house and out from under Emma's feet for a while. My work could be done in the evenings. It was easier and less intense than hers. Emma needed me out of the way so that she could think clearly and even use automated speech software.

Eventually it was Ulf, our pellet supplier, who came up with an answer.

"Here's Ulf, with our pellets", Emma shouted to me. "Can you go and pay him and bring the pellets in? I'm tied up with work at the moment!"

I took the cash – Ulf was always paid in cash but I'm sure it all went through the books in good order, in true Scandinavian style – and went outside to meet him. He gave me a quick wave from the cab of his tractor, delivered two huge pallets of pellets for us and then hopped down to shake my hand, say hello and so forth.

As he got out of the cab I noticed that he was wearing a red and blue scarf, which looked suspiciously like a football scarf.

The only two teams I knew that played in red and blue were Crystal Palace and Barcelona. I couldn't imagine Ulf being a fan of the London club and I wasn't sure about the colours of the latter.

So just as he was about to get back into his cab, curiosity got the better of me and I asked him about the scarf.

"Yes, it is a football scarf", he said, as always with all Swedes, in near perfect English. "It is my club. The football season is ended but we have an important extra game to play now. To see if we will get promotion".

"What's their name?" I asked, "Is it a local club?" I had followed football quite avidly back in Britain but, I suppose like many fans, I'd never given a thought about it in other countries. The likes of Real Madrid or Inter Milan made the sports pages from time to time, but Swedish clubs were never on the back pages of the Sports Argus when I was a lad.

"Östers", said Ulf. "They play in Växjö. We are in the first division this year and now we can go up to the premier league. You should come to the big match!"

After Ulf had gone, I went straight back inside and onto the computer.

Usters? Easters? That was the name that Ulf had used. I didn't know how to spell it but I soon found them thanks to Google. And yes, sure enough, the Swedish football season had just ended for most teams, it being too cold to play during the winter. But Östers, the Växjö based team, had finished in play-off position in their league and were now having a sudden death game against another team to see if they would get promoted or not.

The game also had an extra edge of anticipation, apparently, because it was against Jönköping. That city was actually about 65 miles away but still considered to be one of 'our' local rivals.

I had to go. This looked far too exciting to miss.

As a Midlander, I hadn't experienced much joy in football. All the various English trophies went to teams in Merseyside, London or Manchester. All the same, like any other fan, even when 'my team' wasn't doing very well, I had gone along to plenty of games. As a child I had fond memories of having Bovril and a steak and kidney pie at half time. As an adult the Bovril had given way to a pint of bitter. But then that had been banned. I had also always enjoyed watching the crowds slowly fill a ground as the atmosphere grew and grew. After the game too, seeing the people teeming away through the streets, Lowry like, always seemed exciting. All that and much more went to make for the carnival that is football. It isn't and never has been just about the match itself.

So it was with quite a thrill that I got ready to go to my first ever game in Sweden.

Few Swedish football teams are well known outside of Sweden. For most English fans, the only name they would have been familiar with was Malmö. Way back in the 1980s, Malmo were a big side and reached the final of what is now the Champions League, only to be beaten by Brian Clough's Nottingham Forest.

Despite that relative lack of fame, the game in Sweden was both popular and thriving. And Östers (pronounced more or less as Uss-tess), currently sitting in the second tier of the Swedish league – which was strangely called the first division as is the way with the modern game – had a proud history as one of the best eight or nine teams in the land.

Researching the team further online, I discovered that Östers also had a brand new stadium. It wasn't huge but with a capacity of perhaps 10,000 or so it was certainly handsome. Newly built and largely made out of Swedish timber, and lined with ranks of shiny new red and blue plastic chairs, the ground did the city of Växjö proud.

More than that, the new stadium had a feature that would turn many traditionalist football fans in the UK a shade of envious green; there was, according to the internet, a significant standing section, or terrace, as they are properly called. Which meant that, for the first time since my Dad took me as a child to Aston Villa's ground in Birmingham, I would be able to stand up and watch a football match.

A few days later, with less than half an hour to go before I left the house for the football ground, the sky cleared and the sun once more lit up the October skies.

"Oh look, isn't it beautiful", said Emma.

And it was. It was stunning.

Neither of us had ever been to New England, but, for some reason, the spectacular autumn colours finally illuminated by bright sunshine made us think of that.

"Can I come to the match?" Emma asked suddenly.

Back in the UK, Emma had accompanied me to a few football games, but as that had always been on fine sunny spring day, I had assumed that she had done so just as an excuse to get a few hours' fresh air. But with this being the last game of the season and there being everything to play for, she had decided that this was another game she wanted to come and see.

"Of course you can", I replied. "That would be great. It'd be much more fun with you there!"

Kick off for this final match was 6 pm. And it was a lovely bright sunny afternoon when we set off to go to the game. So much so that neither of us much felt like wearing, or even carrying, thick coats. Fortunately we threw them in the boot of the car anyway.

And how we needed them.

The drive to the game was along empty roads. The car parks near to the ground were half empty too, and for a short while we both wondered if we had got the wrong day or the wrong time.

But within a few minutes' walk of the car, we soon saw crowds wearing the red and blue of Östers and even a few wearing what turned out to be the green and white of Jönköping. The two sets of supporters seemed to mix without any difficulty or hostility.

There's always a sense of anticipation before a football match. The walk to the ground. The gradual convergence of the crowd. It had been a sensation I had first noticed as a child, and it had never grown less. No matter how badly my team usually performed.

Immediately outside the ground, the first real difference I noticed about Swedish football was the food. Before the match and – presumably – at half time, there were no balti pies, no chicken and mushroom pies; not even a steak and kidney pie. There were no chips, no sandwiches, no salads, no kebabs... in fact there was nothing at all except for hot dogs.

By now – after the best part of a year in Sweden – Emma and I had the distinct impression that, for all its positives, the country didn't really seem to offer the world a great deal in terms of food. We had seen huge lumberjack types clambering down from the chunkiest tractors and machines that we had ever seen, only to stop at a wayside cafe for a snack and, thereat, buy and quickly eat the tiniest, most nutritionally challenged snacks in the world. In other words, the hot dog.

The Swedes seemed somehow hooked on these things despite the fact that they were no bigger than a finger, contained no nutrients whatsoever, and were stuck unceremoniously into the thinnest and most dismal looking cheap white rolls I'd ever seen.

If ever there was scope to improve a nation's diet this was it. Entrepreneurs, reach for your super sausage, granary cob and salad. Sweden needs you!

Once inside the ground itself, the second thing I noticed was that everyone seemed to be very quiet.

This didn't worry me at first, as I had already got used to the fact that Swedish people are, generally speaking, a lot quieter than British people. It's quite normal to go into a supermarket that's pretty full and for there to be no more noise than you might hear in a British supermarket when it's shut!

But as kick off approached, and the last glimmers of sunlight faded away, and the floodlights were lit, and the ground filled up to near capacity, it was still much more like a church than a high-pressure football match. And that felt rather surreal. There were about seven thousand people in the ground and it sounded more like seven hundred.

Nor did the noise levels initially increase as the match got underway.

It wasn't that the game was poor. In fact the match began in a fast and furious fashion and, though lacking a little in finesse, wasn't at all short on passion. A lethal looking tackle, by one of 'our' defenders, showed the extent to which this game mattered.

To make things worse in terms of atmosphere, just as a few lads near to us were beginning to sing, a quick early goal by

Jönköping seemed to stop them in their tracks, and for a while I seemed to be the only person in the crowd who was still shouting.

Part of the fun of live football is having a voluble crowd. And if things carried on like this, I was in for a disappointing time.

Fortunately, as Emma pointed out, there was also a ready flow of lager both inside and outside the ground. And as the game wore on, she assured me that voices would undoubtedly be lubricated and tensions, and so noise levels, would mount.

And she was right. As the first half progressed, I began to notice an increasing number of exclamations from the people around us – a kind of "Hai!" sound – every time one of our players was brought down or there was a dubious decision. It sounded rather like a karate tournament was going on somewhere in the stands.

By half time, the score remained Östers 0 - Jönköping 1. And it was time for refreshments. Fifteen minutes later, with meagre hot dogs eaten, coffee and bars of chocolate consumed – and more lager downed – the game resumed with the second half.

And how things changed in that second half.

During the first half, watching people around me drinking alcohol but making no noise, I had come to the conclusion that the beer was weak or possibly even alcohol free.

In fact it was neither.

I don't know how many glasses of beer the average Swede drinks, or whether they are all injected, at birth, with some sort of drug that prevents them feeling the effects before a certain amount of time has passed, but, by the second half, the lager had finally kicked in and the ground had changed from a library into a lion's den.

When I suggested this explanation to Emma afterwards, she suggested that perhaps there was something in the hot dogs. And maybe she was right. Perhaps that was why the horrid things were so popular.

Well, whatever it was, for the rest of the game even more karate-like shouts came from all sides and corners of the ground as every kick and every pass was cheered with increasing passion by the home fans; a crowd which, I noticed, was still continuing to drink.

The sudden award of a corner was met with a cacophony of cries and screams. Loud singing began, too. And even all that was as nothing compared to the wall of noise which erupted when Östers finally found the net from the corner, and equalised. I hadn't heard such a noise at a football ground since Aston Villa scored a home goal against their arch-rivals Birmingham City.

Gone were all vestiges of Scandinavian reserve. At last we had a proper game on our hands.

Sadly, and rather suddenly, midway through the second half, with the game finely poised, an icy airflow arrived to make the October evening bitterly cold.

"Bloody hell, I'm freezing", said Emma, after just a few minutes of the Siberian blast.

I grunted a reply, not wanting to let her know I felt the same.

The game was still going on, but the conditions made me wonder if this was the beginning of a new Ice Age.

An icy mist quickly began to rise from the pitch and I think all of us, everyone in the crowd, began to pity the footballers running around down there in such conditions. And wearing shorts too. I looked at the faces around me, and by now almost every single person was wrapped up in tightly in their scarf with their collars turned up and stamping their feet in a desperate attempt to stay warm. Or even to just stay above freezing point.

Despite its importance, and largely due to the weather, the game was fading away before our very eyes. Then, suddenly, and dramatically, with just a few minutes of the game to go, Östers scored again. And everyone cheered. Clapped. Sang. Jumped up and down, laughed, talked and smiled. Then the final whistle blew.

We had done it. We were promoted.

Not surprisingly, the crowd left the ground pretty smartish. It was just far too cold to hang around on the pitch and celebrate success.

And as Emma and I took a last lingering look at the ground, rapidly disappearing into freezing fog with the sky dark above it, I realised that the late goal had saved us all, players included. Because without it, the game would have gone to extra time. And if that had happened, I'm sure all seven thousand odd of us would have been found frozen in the morning, like one giant ice cube.

Outside the ground, the two sets of supporters – local rivals, it should again be stressed – once more met and mixed with no sign of hostility. That was a nice thing to see.

And the streams of people soon quickly dispersed either back into their homes or into their cars, leaving behind neither litter nor any other mess.

On balance, my first Swedish football match had been a strange experience. A mixture of quiet good manners and loud raw passion. And as I drove back home – and, rightly or wrongly, it's very hard not to think of it – I imagined those mighty Vikings sitting quietly in their wooden houses, making very little noise or mess and not saying boo to a goose. And then, by contrast, going totally berserk when they were unleashed on the shores of Britain. How did they do that? There was no lager back then. Perhaps it was the hot dogs after all.

November

Back in the UK, the common cold and I had often had a very close acquaintance. It frequently paid me visits. Perhaps three, four or even five times a year, without fail, regularly keeping me abreast of all its latest genetic updates. As a child I had been told that such was my lot in life because I lived in the Midlands. It was, so the story went, the cold, flu and bronchitis capital of the UK. For a short while, as industry had disappeared from the area, things had improved. But then, with the increase in car use and over-use of central heating, things had gone downhill once more. The cold and its germs were never very far away.

Suddenly, living in Sweden, all that had changed. It was now November, and I hadn't had a single cold all year. Nothing. Not even a sniffle. Emma, by contrast, had caught two colds, but even those hadn't developed properly.

That was odd. What was going on?

My theory went like this: colds mutate rapidly to suit the local populace. Presumably, the further away you live from your own gene pool, the less likely you are to catch a cold. And if you do catch one, it's less likely to become a full-blown cold. It seemed to make sense.

Emma was from the Isle of Man. She had Danish ancestors. So somewhere, deep inside, she just might be prone to Swedish cold germs. Whereas I was a mixture of English, Scottish, Welsh, German and Spanish! Not a Scandinavian gene in sight. I was almost guaranteed immunity. And that was a nice thought. No more colds for me. Or a lot less of them, anyway.

To be fair, in all probability, neither of us would have noticed that absence of cold germs, or theorised as to the cause, if it hadn't been for the Christmas market.

Back in the summer, when we had been trying to find a studio for Jack the Canadian sculptor, we had come across a wholly surprising mix of farm and industry on a site just outside Växjö. Huseby Bruk, as the place was called, was the site of a gorgeous stately home and gardens. But it was also much more than that. Back in the 1600s, ironworks had been established there to make cannon and the like. Later a blast furnace and foundry had been established. Much of which was still intact and open to the public. It all reminded me very much of Ironbridge in the Severn Valley; the only place I'd ever seen rural industry like that before.

As well as the industry and the stately home, there were also various buildings which had links to forestry and agriculture. Many of which had been built in the 1800s, from what we could gather, by a Swedish man who was the son of an Englishman.

And finally, on top of all that, today there were also various kiosks and stalls. Because in early November every year, Huseby

Bruk was also the home of the largest Christmas market in Scandinavia.

Attracting around 30,000 visitors, with over 150 exhibitors, Huseby Christmas market was apparently a must-see. According to the advertising material, there would be hand-made products of all kinds, from reindeer wool jumpers to traditional wooden dolls. Also, various types of food, most of it produced on a very small scale. "And surely that", Emma said, as she read the text aloud, "must mean it's better quality than the stuff in the supermarkets and restaurants?" In addition to that, as far as we could tell there would be demonstrations in candle-making, basket-making, carving, woodworking... all sorts of things.

All in all, it sounded like the perfect Christmas market. Nothing fake. Traditional materials. Handicrafts. A rural site, set amongst fine gardens and old industrial buildings.

And what really sold me on the idea was the following sentence: 'Enjoy all the aromatic scents of juniper, wax candles, good food, mulled wine...'

"I've got a cold", I said miserably, on the morning of the market. "My first one. And I'm completely blocked up". Only two days before, we had talked to some English people we had met in a supermarket in Växjö. They were as surprised as we were to find other Brits living in Kronoberg. But one of them had just come back from the UK, and had had a cold...

The market was on for nine days and open until 8 pm every evening, by which time it was very, very dark in Sweden in November. So on witnessing my misery, Emma suggested that we hold off going to the market for a few days and wait for my cold to get a little better. There was no rush.

That sounded a good idea. But a check on the weather forecast made us decide to stick with our original plan. Because from tomorrow onwards, for the first time in months, it was going to rain. And we didn't want to walk around a candlelit market festooned with Christmas lights, dashing from cover to cover in the rain and mud. So cold or not, we would go today.

"I'll let you know which bits smell wonderful. And what they smell of", Emma laughed unsympathetically, as we set off in the car for the market later that day.

It was only half an hour or so by car, but by the time we got to Huseby, it was already completely dark. And – very unusually for Swedish roads – we even found ourselves sitting in a traffic jam, albeit a shortish one that did keep slowly moving.

"All of these must going to the market", said Emma, who was driving.

I looked ahead and, sure enough, the vast majority of the cars were indicating left to turn off the main road for the official car park.

Admission to the market was a very reasonable 100 krona – or about 10 pounds sterling. But to our huge surprise, the car parking was free. And – even more surprisingly – entrance to the market for children under 12 was also free.

"Well, we're certainly not in England now", I said as we noticed the prices – or, rather, lack of prices. "It would be £15 to park in the UK. At least £10 for kids and at least £20 or more for adults."

"And people back home think Sweden's expensive", said Emma. "A failed socialist experiment".

We laughed, paid, and went in.

Had I been about five or six years old, the sight of Huseby Bruk that night would have instilled a life-long belief in fairies and magic and Father Christmas. It looked fantastic.

Small wooden kiosks, lit with a warm glow. Outdoor candles, situated here and then, flickering and sputtering in the night air. Christmas lights, people wearing fur coats..

"So go on then", I snuffled, "Does it really all smell of juniper and mulled wine?"

Emma sniffed the air and nodded. "Yes. It does. It really does. It smells fantastic. Just like you might expect Christmas to smell".

The first stall we visited sold handmade fur hats. All reindeer fur. All environmentally and sustainably... etc. etc. Assuming that reindeer herding itself was those things too. We had no idea. I tried on a grey hat, immediately feeling as warm and comfortable as if I was asleep back home in bed with a duvet pulled over my head. But, style wise, it just wasn't me.

Inside a long low wooden hut, illuminated with low-key white lights, we looked at all kinds of pieces of carved wood and handmade candles, and then found ourselves next to hand-made reindeer sausages too.

"Presumably, these are the ones that provide the fur for the hats outside," said Emma.

A huge Swede – or perhaps he was a Sami, one of the Laplanders who herd reindeer for a living – offered us a piece of one of the sausages. I took it a little gingerly, not because it was made of deer, but because this was Sweden and, so far, food here had not been very good.

This sausage *was* good. Smoked, of course, as everything here seemed to be, and a little too salty, but underneath that, the flavour was good, and the meat was very good quality for once.

A little further on, we had our first glass of mulled wine. The night was cold but, sadly, snowless. (It was only early November). All the same, a glass of wine would help keep the chill out. And, according to the woman behind the stall, it would help me get rid of my cold too.

And it did do that. She was right. At least briefly. I nearly choked on the overpowering flavours of the wine, but after that initial shock, the cinnamon rush went straight into battle with my cold germs. I could feel it. And for a while at least, I could breathe clearly and even smell the real wax candles. A fine smell.

From the wine stall we went into the former foundry.

"Wow!" said Emma. She had studied industrial archaeology at university and always loved discovering somewhere new of interest.

Although the roof and other parts of the building were fully or partially restored, the original vast stone fireplace, which must have been the furnace, was still intact.

It was pretty impressive, and all the more so with the Christmas stalls set out around it, giving the whole place the feel of a Victorian Christmas.

Later, with yet more mulled wine, and some very nice (but smoked) cheese and ham inside us, we looked around the millrace too. This was another fascinating piece of working industrial heritage.

By now the crowds were starting to dissipate, and although we hadn't bought anything for Christmas, we had tried a few foods and Emma had gone back and bought some reindeer sausages. We decided it was time to go, too. It had turned much colder and my own cold was creeping back up on me again.

But we promised ourselves another visit, probably in the summer, to look at the site again. In terms of tangible heritage, it really was the most interesting place we had found so far in Sweden.

*

Mid November was bleak. I had once seen a documentary about Iceland, a country I had always – prior to that documentary – wanted to visit. The landscape looked fascinating. The idea of bathing outdoor in hot water springs appealed hugely. But not once, during the whole programme, did the sun appear. Not once was there a gap in the leaden grey skies. Now Sweden was doing the same thing. Only, thanks to the wall of skog, it was even darker. Daytime came and went without registering. We had our lights on indoors from the moment we got out of bed to the moment we returned to it.

And it didn't just last for one day. Or two. Or three. Ten days had passed without a single glimpse of sunlight. And without even five minutes of sunlight, we both had the skin colour of boiled cod. Our summer tans were already a distant memory.

But at least it wasn't just us. Jack the Canadian called down one afternoon, and he looked even paler than we did. Edvard too, despite his centuries of Scandinavian genes, was fed up with the grey and – for once – looked all of his 80 plus years.

It was as dark as that, and yet it wasn't wet. Apart from the first week of November, when it had rained, the skies were simply grey and dry. No snow. No sleet. Nothing. It was as if the whole world had become encased in a steel shell with a matt grey undercoat.

"You know", I said to Emma one morning, as we sat and ate breakfast looking out at the sullen cloud overhead. "I'd never really realised it before. Never given it a thought. But Sweden is very much somewhere to spend summer outdoors. As much as possible. At every available opportunity. And then, once the warm weather has gone, to spend as much time as possible indoors".

Emma nodded. "I know what you mean. You really do have to get out, out and then out a bit more in the nicer months. It never really mattered in England. But here it's completely different in that respect. It's an outdoor country. And then an indoor country."

"I can see why they all take holidays mid-winter in Thailand too", I said, finishing off my tea and doing a few dishes.

We went back to our laptops, with work to do and emails to answer. It was the time of year to do indoor things. But what, apart from work, did that consist of?

As if by magic, an answer arrived.

"What's a hyttsill?" I shouted through from my office to where Emma was sitting in hers.

"No idea", she shouted back.

I'd just begun to google the word when Emma came into the room. "Why?" she asked.

"We've got an invite to go to a hyttsill, from Anders and Linda".

We looked it up.

Apparently a hyttsill was a 'hot shop herring'. I looked up at Emma. She shrugged her shoulders.

"A long time ago, in the glass blowing region of Småland...." I began.

"Here", said Emma.

"Yes, here.. Anyway, it says that a long time ago, tramps, vagabonds, whatever, used to wander around the countryside telling stories to earn a bit of food and a night in a warm bed. One of the places they liked to aim for was the glass-blowing room in one of the glass factories. Because the furnaces were often in use all night, or at least kept lit all night. The men working there would give them some food and a bed by the furnace in return for telling a story or singing a ballad".

I paused. Skimmed through some more of the text.

"And. So. Today... the tradition lives on. After the end of a day's work, the glass blowers go home. But the glass blowing studio, presumably still warmed by the furnace, is turned into a sort of restaurant".

Emma made a harumphing noise.

"Hmm. Yeah, I know what you mean. It probably won't be good food. Stale herrings with too much sugar and too much dill. But. But... there's beer. And apparently we all sit at long wooden trestle tables and someone recites old Swedish stories and there's singing". I finished reading the stuff off the internet and went back to my email. "So, really, we should go. Give it a try". I said, waiting for Emma's response before I replied to Anders and Linda.

"We should", Emma agreed. "And, anyway, it'll be a night out. We were just saying that winter's for indoor things".

The hyttsill would be at Kosta glassworks, in ten days, and we already knew the village of Kosta itself.

Thanks to the resurgence of the glass industry in the area, Kosta had recently expanded into a large village with an ultra-modern art hotel, as well as a factory outlet shopping centre. Emma and I had visited the shops there to buy clothes – big labels at cheap prices – on a few occasions. And we had enjoyed it. But we had stopped doing that, more or less, once we had discovered a charity shop in nearby Nybro which sold nearly new clothes with Stockholm labels. The prices there were just unbelievably low.

The glassworks themselves, however, we had not yet been to. And even before the mail from Anders, Emma and I had felt a bit bad about that; all the more so after we had failed to really discover the emigrant trail back in the summer. Sweden did have a lot of heritage on offer. And if we were going to make it our permanent home, we needed to get out and discover more of it. After all, we were living in Kronoberg. And Kronoberg was the centre of Swedish glass. Glasriket, in Swedish. (Literally 'The Kingdom of Glass'.)

Handmade glass. Coloured glass. Blown glass. Glass vases, glass bowls, glass trophies. Everything. If it's made from glass, or if it can be made in glass, it would be made here. Somewhere or other.

There were a score of glass factories, too, scattered throughout the region. Fewer now than there had been once, but still quite a number. And today, more than ever, these were popular places for tourists. Some were situated in the forest beside a stream; small glassworks, producing a few pieces each year. Others – such as the one in Kosta – were located in villages. Sometimes the settlement grew up around the glass manufacturing, sometimes the glassworks were built in a semi-urban area.

And Sweden was like that. Wherever you went, industry and housing were mixed shoulder to shoulder. It seemed to be a land of entrepreneurs and small businesses. Or maybe people just didn't want to commute too far in snowy conditions. It was probably a bit of both. Usually it worked. But sometimes – as with the chicken factory in Karlshamn and the huge ugly grain silos we had seen in the coastal resort of Åhus – it didn't.

The problem for us, however, was that neither of us had any passion or interest in glass. We admired the industry for its history. All the more so because it had remained here, in the countryside, rather than moving to one of the big cities or industrial estates somewhere. The craftsmanship too, we appreciated. But glass as a substance? No. For some reason, it did nothing for either of us. Something to drink out of or to keep the milk in. But otherwise? No. Not really.

Be that as it may, by the night of the 'hot shop herring', Emma and I were both looking forward to it hugely. The truth was that the timing was ideal; we needed a break. The dismal depressing grey still hadn't moved, so we had taken on extra work and spent the whole of the last week sitting indoors, in the gloom, working at our computers. We were fed up with that, and a night out in good company was the ideal remedy.

We met Anders and Linda outside Kosta glassworks. The building itself was non-descript although a sign on the end wall showed just how long glass had been playing a major role in this part of Sweden; the works had been established in 1742.

Anders and Linda looked like they had just spent a day on the beach, sunbathing and probably surfing. But of course this being November, and the Baltic already hovering around a chilly 6 °C or so, they had actually been doing neither.

They had brought along two more friends with them – both Swedish – who they had just taken on as employees. And Emma and I were introduced to Per and Anna.

"I thought you said it was too expensive to hire staff in Sweden!"

"Oh well, we have just won a huge contract", Linda replied.

Anders nodded and laughed. "And of course we will be firing these two just as soon as they have helped make us very rich!" Per and Anna grinned.

Other people were going into the factory, and we followed them. "You'll love this", said Anders, holding the door for us. "I promise".

Once inside, we were pleased to see that there had been no attempt at all to disguise or change the nature of the furnace room. It was a functional space where glass was still being blown in the daytime. And at night, from time to time, the factory was being used for herring suppers.

All the same, an effort had been made to try to turn the clock back a hundred years or so, to the time where itinerants would sing or tell jokes for their supper. There were long wooden tables, candles and the fire was lit in the furnace. Outside it was dark; inside it was warm and inviting.

We were all seated at one candlelit table, and found ourselves sharing it with some other Swedes. None of us knew them, but we all said hello and introduced ourselves anyway. It was normal to do that in Sweden. First names are a must.

And then the night got going as the food and drink began to appear – and disappear – in earnest.

The food was pretty much as expected. Sill (herring) in several flavours, most of which weren't very good, but one or two were quite reasonable. Which was nice, because in theory sill ought to be a really tasty – and healthy – dish. So perhaps it's time will come again.

There was also an assortment of (smoked) cheese, (smoked) ham and even (unsmoked!) boiled eggs. A bit of salad. And some good sourdough bread.

Maybe it was sharing the experience with friends, or maybe it was that we were becoming acclimatised to Swedish food, but somehow both Emma and I even cleared our plates.

The beer certainly helped. It wasn't strong. But there was enough of it to wash down some of the smokiness of the food. Certainly the polite levels of conversation that had been the rule in the room to begin with were gradually becoming more voluble. People were talking, laughing and even conversing with strangers.

Then, suddenly, from the back of the room, a set of bagpipes started playing. And hands started clapping as the piper appeared then paraded around the room a few times, still playing.

Anders assured us that the tune was a very well-known folk song, and sure enough, after a few minutes some voices started to sing along to it.

After that, on the little stage set in the corner of the room, musicians dressed in old-time clothes began to strum guitars and sing what sounded to us rather maudlin songs. To the Swedes in the room, however, these were calls to action or, at least, calls to sing along. And soon everyone, including Linda, Anders, Pers and Anna, was joining in.

There were a few gaps, during which some jokes were told or a longish story was recited. The jokes went down well and some of the stories even had a few people in the audience dabbing their eyes.

All in all it was a very entertaining evening. And one which showed us a different side to the Swedish character. They were a rather sad people, albeit in the nicest way, with lots of respect for tradition and an almost repressed urge to sing in public. Almost. We had neither of us forgotten how attached they were to Eurovision.

Certainly it was something we would do again, unlike our visits to Swedish restaurants. The only real regret we had was that, although both of us spoke some Swedish, we didn't understand either the jokes or the songs and Linda had to explain them to us.

"You must learn it better", said Anders.

He was right, of course. No matter how well the Swedish spoke English, learning the language fully – or as fully as possible – would also help make Sweden into our permanent home.

*

A few days after the hyttsill evening, Emma came back from the village shop with some good news; news directly tied to our night out with the herrings.

She had been to the shop to buy a few odds and ends, but also to post a parcel to the Isle of Man. As ever, despite Carina's many skills, she hadn't been able to figure out the correct postage. And so Emma had done it for her while Carina had taken a break.

Emma had joined Carina for a coffee and cake, sitting in the little cafe-like corner of the shop. And they had got to talking about life in Sweden, how we were finding it, and so forth.

Emma had told Carina about the hyttsill. And about the jokes, songs and stories.

"Oh yes", Carina had agreed. "That sounds very familiar. Swedish people love to sing. And even if we are happy at first, if we have had a few drinks, our songs do become a bit slow and sad. It is the forest. I think".

The conversation had drifted around to language, and Emma had asked Carina whether she knew of anyone in the area who offered Swedish language lessons.

"Well", said Carina. "There are free courses for all immigrants. I know that. The government arrange these and they are very good. So that people who move here are not left out. You can go to take one of those. In Växjö there will be a course. But..."

"But?"

"But maybe I can help you and you can help me".

The long and the short of it was that, for a few hours a week, Carina would be happy to teach us Swedish in return for us, or one of us, teaching her children some basic English. They were only young, but she wanted them to get a head start before starting school. Would we be interested?

It sounded ideal.

More than ideal.

"I'll be happy to do that", I said.

"I knew you would be", Emma laughed. "I've already told Carina that you'll do it for her".

I was going to end my first year in Sweden as a teacher. Of sorts. Carina was one of the nicest people I had ever met. Outgoing, helpful and friendly. And, of course, the blonde hair and blue eyes helped persuade me, too.

So as the end of November arrived we had our first Swedish lesson.

A long time ago, at university, I had studied the language a little. And I was surprised how quickly some of the basics came back to me. Emma was a natural with languages anyway, so she picked it up easily.

The truth is that Swedish isn't a particularly difficult language to learn. Verb endings are easy, for example, with just one form – unlike French. And there's a tendency in the language to say things as simply as possible. To keep the number of words down. And in those ways it is very like English. A language for instructions rather than romance, perhaps. But if it makes it easier to learn...

The hardest part is hearing the words, and sometimes compound words, which – when spoken – tend to blur into one another. And then there are accents. Carina spoke clearly, as did most people in Kronoberg. But in the south of Sweden, nearer to Denmark, we hadn't ever been able to understand a single word.

Like everything else in life, it surely come with practice. The most important thing was to try.

December

The year had begun with snow. And at the end of the year, December began in exactly the same way. We woke up to find a heavily yellow sky filled with great fat flakes of snow. Our drive was already covered – albeit to a shallow depth so far. And more, much more, was being forecast by the radio to arrive during the course of the next 48 hours.

In a way – in many ways – it was ideal.

Despite the almost remorseless nature of the stuff, and the fact that it changed the way we lived, and despite the fact that we were new to such winter wonderland weather, we actually enjoyed the snow.

Once the leaves of autumn had gone, and the dark, dark days of late October and November had arrived, Sweden had been transformed from a cheerfully bright place into a rather drab and depressing one. Amongst its many other qualities, the snow changed that. With a white carpet on the land, and trees, the outdoors once more became a bright and cheerful place. We had already realised that winter, so far north, would be an awfully dismal experience without snow. So we were glad to see it.

On top of that, of course, it was December, and there were only a few weeks to Christmas.

As children, we had seen perhaps two or three 'white' Christmases. And one or two of those were really little more than a centimetre of snow, or perhaps just a very harsh frost. This year, for sure, we were going to get the real thing. And that was a wonderfully cheering thought.

We had no children, and we weren't expecting any guests, but Emma and I still enjoyed celebrating Christmas in our own way. We always had a tree, some decorations and candles, and we also made sure we had plenty of wine, good food and cake or chocolates too. We would switch off the computers for a few days, and sit and eat, drink, and watch old black and white films.

Talking about that, as we watched the snow fall, we realised that this Christmas, even though we would have the snow, we might struggle to find the right kind of food and drink.

There was only one answer. A quick call to Johan to book a drive clearing for the next morning, and a short away day to Copenhagen, our nearest big city and, of course, not a Swedish one (so hopefully better food and drink!)

The drive to Copenhagen was quite long, about three hours. And yet, although we drove past Malmö – one of the three big cities in Sweden – it was still much closer to us than any other large urban space.

For some reason, Malmö didn't really appeal to either Emma or me. We had been there once, because of some problem with opening a bank account. And the centre of the city, to our eyes, just wasn't very appealing. Lots of buildings of about eight stories, often made of brick, some covered with plaster. A grid like system of roads. And a cold, wind tunnel-like effect. Of course that had been in January, so we were almost certainly being unfair to the city. Pretty much everywhere at the time was cold and had a bitter strong wind blowing. And it was hard to stop and appreciate the architecture when bent almost double in a big coat, desperate to get out of the biting temperatures and dashing from the car to the warmth of a bank.

Researching it online, there were actually some very nice buildings in the place and so we promised ourselves to give it another try. One day. But not yet. Today we were on the ring road around Malmö and, once more, it looked a pretty bleak place.

The Swedish forest runs out about 40 km north of Malmö. From that point down to the coast, there are flat, exposed looking fields; a Sweden that looks more like the Fens of Cambridgeshire than the forest we were already becoming accustomed to. And the ring road more or less exacerbated the effect, giving the false impression – especially in winter – of Sweden having a featureless and harsh land.

All the same, as we sped along the road in the direction of the Öresund Bridge which connects Denmark to Sweden and so, in effect, Copenhagen to Malmö, we did notice some huge new out-of-town developments, including a massive IKEA store. And so we agreed that we really must give Malmö another try in the not-too-distant future.

Then, suddenly, we could see the big bridge.

This huge and impressive construction – part bridge and part tunnel under the sea – has made a massive difference to Scandinavia and, in particular, to Sweden.

In so many ways, judging by what we had heard and seen, this single structure had done more than thousands of years of history to open up Sweden to the rest of the world. And the region between the two countries, the two cities, the region of the bridge, was now one of the most prosperous places in the world. The economy was booming. People commuted between the two sides. Advances in industry, technology and more were made here at an alarming rate.

The bridge had also already been the centrepiece of a TV crime series. A gloomy affair, from what few clips we had seen, which made Sweden and Denmark both look like they were set permanently in November and everyone, everywhere, was involved in narcotics smuggling or worse.

There was some truth in it, no doubt. After all, Copenhagen in particular was a very big city. And where there's money, there is always crime. But it was also very, very far removed from the Sweden we had been living in, the one where most Swedes lived.

And, at the end of the day, good TV programme or not, it was drama, not fact.

As we crossed the bridge, without needing to show passports or any such inconvenience, the sea – at this point, a narrow channel between Denmark and Sweden called the Öresund Strait – seemed to be a very long way beneath us. And it didn't look very inviting either, with white foam flecked waves and a greenish grey colour. Emma, who was driving, didn't look at it. She was prone to sea sickness, and the sea today was definitely in that kind of mood.

But we were soon in the tunnel, and then passing Copenhagen international airport, with a plane coming into land just over our heads, and within a few more minutes we were parking in the city itself.

At first, because the drive had been quite long, we parked overlooking the sea, facing across the water towards Malmö and Sweden. Copenhagen is a port, although these days it seems to mainly handle cruise ships rather than freight. And the sea front is now a popular place with joggers, cyclists and – at the right time of the year – swimmers too.

We walked along for a few hundred metres, as far as a large wooden structure resembling a skeletal Roman arena, the wooden framework giving it an unfinished appearance. To our surprise, despite the fact that it was almost mid-December, and the sea was an angry green, two portly gentlemen, who looked as if they were in their 70s, were climbing out of the water and onto the wooden structure where they dried themselves off cheerfully.

Personally, and despite being a good 25 years younger, I wouldn't have wanted to put even my hand in the sea. It looked freezing.

A short while later, we moved the car to the edge of the city centre so that we could do some Christmas shopping.

In places Copenhagen is a strikingly pretty city, full of life and full of people who seem to be doing very nicely. Regular surveys show the Danish to be the happiest people in the world.

And as we walked along, although we hadn't been in Sweden for long, we figured we could already tell the difference between a Swede and a Dane. The Danes had paler complexions. Their blonde hair was sandier. And – true to those survey results – they also seemed to smile more.

Of course those were just generalisations, but as we popped in and out of an assortment of shops, buying odds and ends, it did seem to be a cheery kind of place.

Eventually we decided that we needed to take a break. To stop off and have a drink in a bar or cafe. We found a small, brick lined place, with jazz music playing. Unlike in Sweden there was a huge range of drink on offer and – also unlike anywhere else in Europe – there were people smoking in the bar.

"Is that legal?" Emma wondered. Although neither of us were smokers, it didn't bother us that others were.

That was an odd thing about the Danes. They were in the EU, but appeared to regularly bend or alter rules to suit their own circumstances. Unlike the Swedes, who seemed to be sticklers for the law, the Danes liked to be different. So they worked with the European rules they liked, and opted out of the rest. It wasn't a dictatorship, after all. There was always scope to do that. And the Danes did it readily.

Back outside, the sky was already turning dark. In Scandinavia, the sun goes down very late in the summer. But the downside to that is that it sets very early in the winter.

We walked along admiring the Christmas lights and then headed out of town to a large German owned chain store to fill the boot of the car with wine. Once more, this was much more readily available in Denmark than it was in Sweden.

"Copenhagen was nice", said Emma, as I drove us back over the bridge, the water underneath now dark. We had been to Copenhagen before, but only on fleeting visits. That had been our first proper visit. "I'm glad we have such a big city close by".

"Me too".

Suddenly we were back in Sweden. And on the now almost empty ring road around Malmö.

"All the same", Emma added. "I'm glad we live in the forest!"

Once clear of the Malmö region, and off the main roads and driving through the forest, the night was staggeringly beautiful. Every now and then, a small cottage would appear in the trees, with plain white or simple yellow Christmas lights, usually in the form of candelabras or stars placed in every window.

It was incredibly picturesque.

I had been brought up in a big city myself. And I wouldn't have wanted to change that, even if it were possible to do so. For me, growing up offered all sorts of opportunities. That's what big cities are for.

All the same, now being in my early 50s, I wouldn't want to go back there to live. And I agreed with Emma – being back in the forest already felt like home.

*

Although we had bought most of our Christmas food and drink in Copenhagen, we still had to buy something for Christmas dinner itself. Neither Emma nor I had ever eaten goose, as it had always seemed far too expensive and even excessive, given that there were only two of us. But this year, with the snow already forming a blanket over the world, and our first Christmas in Sweden, it just seemed to be the ideal dinner. It felt right.

Besides, there was no real choice in the supermarkets.

Denmark may have a reasonable range of products; it's attached to Germany, which means it's attached directly to Europe. But Sweden is more, well, standoffish. And in some supermarkets, it's still difficult to find a whole chicken, never mind anything more elaborate than that.

The Swedes themselves – and neither Emma nor I knew how they did it – ate meatballs, smoked ham and spare ribs at Christmas. Just as they ate meatballs, smoked ham and spare ribs at Easter. And just as they ate meatballs, smoked ham and spare ribs throughout the year. Their diet seemed to be monotonous and not very exciting, especially as the meatballs, ham and spare ribs were such poor quality.

We did have the impression that things were slowly changing, though, and that a wider variety of foods was slowly becoming acceptable. But producers were still limited, the state still controlled too much in terms of production, and – as we had found throughout the year – stuff like salt and sugar were still used in an over-abundance.

Nevertheless, for some reason, geese – and affordable geese at that! – found their way into the supermarkets as Christmas approached. Not a great number of them, and if you didn't buy one when they first appeared, you might not get one at all. But they were there.

And so we went out in search of our Christmas dinner.

Of course normally buying food from a supermarket is pretty straightforward. But this was Sweden and odd things seemed to happen here all the time...

Sweden is in the EU but not part of the Eurozone. And that means it still uses its own currency and its own banknotes. One of these, the highest denomination, is for 1,000 Swedish kronor (abbreviated as kr or sometimes SEK). And this is approximately equivalent to 100 pounds sterling.

It was nearly closing time when we arrived in the supermarket. And the aisles – which were never very full in Sweden – were almost empty.

Initially we were only going to buy a goose, but once we saw how empty the shop was, we went back and collected a shopping trolley, filling it up as we went with numerous items and self-scanning them as we did so.

At one point Emma was unsure which dairy produce to buy, and as she hesitated over her choice, I walked around to the bread counter. It was largely empty except for a couple of sourdough loaves. I had picked up both of those, thinking that we could freeze one of them, when I saw a banknote on the floor.

I bent down to pick it up and saw two more things. Both of which surprised me. The first was that it was a 1,000 kr note. I had just found about 100 GBP on the floor of the supermarket. The second was that this note wasn't an orphan. There was another. And another. And another.

Naturally I couldn't believe what I was seeing.

Along the aisle where I was standing, together with tins of peaches and tins of sardines in a horrible cheap tomato sauce, there were a couple of dozen of these bank notes. Lying there, for all the world, like litter. As if someone had just got fed up carrying them and had scattered them on the floor out of boredom.

Instinctively I looked up, half expecting to see a hidden television camera, or a policeman, or a shop assistant with a hessian sack full of cash and a large hole in the bottom of it. But there were none of those things.

At that moment Emma appeared around the corner with the trolley, self-scanning an item as she did so.

"Look". I said. Not too loud, but loud enough for her to hear. And I pointed at the floor.

Emma's eyes widened, and her mouth opened. But she didn't say a word.

Then – having always been quicker than me at spotting a bargain – she pounced on the banknotes and scooped them up 'like a tramp on chips', as the saying goes.

And coming finally to my senses, I did the same.

"Oh my god", she said, as we pocketed the last of them. "How much is there here? What should we do?"

Both questions were very much at the front of my mind too.

For the next few minutes, as we pretended to carefully verify the contents of a tin of frankfurter sausages, the likes of which we would never buy, we checked and double-checked the loot we had just found.

"There's about 30,000 kr in total". I concluded. "Three grand, in English money".

We shuffled around the shop, popping items almost randomly into the trolley. Although very distracted, we did remember to pick up a goose. But I was pretty sure we'd forgotten to scan at least one thing. Somehow it didn't seem important.

"What shall we do?" Emma asked. Or I asked. Probably both of us said it several times.

Probably, in another place, back in the UK, or even anywhere other than Sweden, we might well have just decided 'finders keepers'. But here, in our adopted country, in a land where people were trusted rather than doubted, where we already had friends – people who were always polite and generous – where stuff could be left in the garden without it being stolen, where even boats could be left beside a lake without anyone damaging them... we both came to same conclusion. "We have to hand it all in", said Emma.

I agreed. It was the right thing to do. Christmas spirit. All that sort of thing.

"OK", I said. "Yes. I think that's best. You hand it in. But I can't bear to watch. I'll pay for this lot while you do it".

Fifteen minutes later, Emma finally appeared outside. I had bought and paid for our shopping and put it in the boot of the car.

"Done?" I asked.

"Done", she replied. "They've taken my name and address and said that they'll look into it. They have no idea how the money got there".

"Well", I said, as we drove away. "At least it pays to be honest". Emma nodded, and we drove off in silence.

"What do you mean, it pays to be honest?" she said at last.

We were at a set of red traffic lights. I looked up at them and then across at her. "What with one thing and another, with all that money and neither of us sure what to do about it, I think we forgot to scan half of the stuff we put in the trolley".

The lights changed and I drove off.

"The goose too?" asked Emma.

I nodded.

We had avoided buying one before because they were so expensive. This year we had decided to get one anyway. But we'd never expected to get the damned thing for nothing!

*

One of our favourite films, and something we tried to watch most Christmases, was Frank Capra's 'It's a Wonderful Life'. Starring James Stewart and Donna Reed, it must be one of the most touching films ever made. A heart-warming tale about a man who always does the right thing and who then gets overwhelmed by life. In the end, after several tear-jerking scenes, it all comes out right.

We loved the film, having both watched it many times as children.

Ironically, snow plays a key role in the film. Not only do flakes of snow signal to the main protagonist that he is 'back' in his own world, and safe, but a thick blanket of Christmas snow lying across the sleepy town of Bedford Falls is also used to portray the difference between a 'good town' and the ghastly, grasping alternative.

As I looked out of the window, on Christmas Eve – our first Christmas Eve in Sweden – I was disappointed to see that the skies remained stubbornly grey. And equally stubbornly free of snow.

No snow had fallen since the start of the month.

Our first – and supposedly almost guaranteed – white Christmas in Sweden was not going to be a white one after all.

"Come on", said Emma, "Or we'll be late".

A week earlier, we had called in to visit our bank, which was in a pretty village called Hovmantorp.

Hovmantorp was situated on a lake and consisted of a few shops, a few low-rise blocks of flats and a railway station. But other than that, a population of about 2,000 lived mainly in amongst the trees, in a scattering of detached wooden houses.

As was typical in rural Sweden, most of those homes were fairly small. Although this was a huge country, and every property stood on its own land, Emma and I guessed that houses were often small because it was generally cheaper and easier to heat a small house. They were often self-built too, and that was probably easier to do on a smaller scale.

Nevertheless, one or two homes in Hovmantorp were larger than the others, and more ornate too. So much so that they looked for all the world like the big old house in that James Stewart film. The one that's derelict at the start of the film, and into which he moves with his wife and children.

Even the church had a Mid-West American feel to it. Covered in pale custard coloured plaster, highlighted with white, it looked like something off a wedding cake, or possibly from a film set. All that was missing was the white picket fencing, and a house just a few doors away had some of that!

In short, Hovmantorp was an idyllic Swedish village. Or very very small town. And Emma and I both found it to be very attractive.

Our business in the bank concluded, we had bought a few things from the supermarket, and then – just as we were about to leave – Emma had spotted a small sign on the noticeboard of the supermarket.

"Oh look", she said, "We must go to that. Christmas Eve, at midnight, a candlelit mass at the church. Here in Hovmantorp".

I read the notice over her shoulder.

Neither of us were religious in the churchgoing sense, but midnight mass, by candlelight, seemed too nice an opportunity to miss. Apart from anything else, it would allow us to see yet another side of the Swedish.

So it was that on Christmas Eve, with the sky dark but stubbornly snowless, we set off for the 20-minute drive to Hovmantorp.

We set off a little early as we had planned to take a short walk beside the inky black waters of the lake, before going to the mass.

It must have been around 10.30 pm when we parked the car in the main, almost deserted, car park in Hovmantorp. We got out of the car, and walked across the railway line to the shore of the lake. We had no particular reason for wanting to take a walk along the sand; it wasn't something we normally did at this time of year, but I think we both felt that a few minutes to just savour the complete peace and quiet was a good idea. The right thing to do at this time of year.

Warmly clad against the cold night air, we walked along the narrow beach, beside the silent water of the lake, for about 15 minutes. Then we turned and walked back towards the village centre.

By now we could see that there were a few other cars in the car park. And that felt a bit of a relief. I think both of us might have been a little uncomfortable if we had gone into the mass almost on our own. Truth be told, we probably wouldn't have gone in at all.

Suddenly it happened. From the still night sky overhead, one big fat flake of snow fell, landing right on my nose.

Then another.

And another.

And soon, before we had even got as far as the car park, it was snowing heavily. With the same 'I'm gonna cover everything' attitude that it had shown in January as we had struggled (and failed) to clear our drive with a snow blower.

"Oh, isn't that perfect?" said Emma.

And it was.

There was still the best part of an hour to go before midnight. And although we could go into the church already, we decided to leave it a little while longer, and sat in the car, watching winter arrive on Christmas Eve.

By the time we got out of the car, an incredibly thick layer of snow already lay over everything.

"It looks just like Bedford Falls", said Emma, clinging onto me as much as I was clinging onto her, as we walked up the path towards the church.

I paused and looked around. She was right. It did.

Hovmantorp, with its wooden houses, broad empty streets, old trees and tidy fences, had turned into Frank Capra's 'Bedford Falls'.

It couldn't have looked nicer. It couldn't have been more appropriate.

"It's a wonderful life!" I laughed.

And we went into the church.

The interior of the church was much starker than we had imagined. Sweden is a Lutheran country. And from what I could gather, that seemed to mean few paintings, and decorating all the walls with simple colours; white, pale blue, gold.

Despite that lack of character, however, tonight, lit only by candles, the simple Lutheran interior glittered and sparkled with a dreamlike quality.

Emma and I wanted to take two places near the back of the church, to keep out of the way a bit. But as it was already very busy and, from what we could see, almost full, and as a lot of Swedes had had the same idea – to stay near the back, out of the way – we were politely ushered to the front of the church.

We said a quiet hello to the woman sitting next to us and took our place. And then the service started.

We discovered that Swedish church services resembled English church services. They were quiet. There were hymns. And the priest (or vicar – we had no idea what the proper title was) spoke for a while.

Periodically I glanced out of the windows, past the flickering candles, and could see that the snow was still falling.

It certainly felt like Christmas.

Then the priest turned his attention to the woman seated next to us. And she got up and went to the front of the church, where there was a small low stage.

Clearly she was going to sing.

"I'm sure I recognise her from somewhere", Emma whispered as the woman began to sing a slow and soulful tune.

Her voice was superb. And it seemed to perfectly suit the mood and night. But more than that, she seemed completely confident. Not once did she lose her poise; not once – in three songs – did her voice waver or break.

It was superb. Wonderfully well done.

Then she resumed her seat next to us. And after a few more spoken words, the service was over. And people started to stand and gather their things to leave.

"I have to say something..." Emma said to me. And with that she turned to the woman, who had just finished speaking to an older couple on her other side.

"Excuse me", said Emma, "But I have to say, your singing was really quite beautiful. And you seemed so calm".

She turned to us and smiled. "Thank you", she said. "But can I ask you, are you English, by any chance?"

"Yes we are", Emma replied. "But we live here now. Well, not far from here. We've been living in Sweden for about a year".

Her smile widened still further. "Oh, well, in that case, welcome to Sweden", she said.

We spoke for a minute or two more. Emma described roughly where we lived. And the woman said she knew it, and that she had played nearby as a child.

We left the service to find ourselves, just after midnight on Christmas morning, faced with a scene straight from a Christmas card. The whole village was tucked under a thick blanket of snow. The snow had stopped falling. But everything, everywhere, was white. It was a wonderful sight.

"She was so nice", said Emma as we walked back to the car. "And I'm sure I've seen her before somewhere".

I agreed. She was nice. And there was indeed something strangely familiar about her.

It was a bit of a mystery. And we had to wait a few more days before it was solved.

*

Christmas Day and Boxing Day came and went without any disturbance, passing in a bit of a blur. We ate as much of the goose as we could, drank more wine than we ought to have done and watched any old films we could find. And by the 27th of December we were back at work on our laptops.

Outside, things had remained grey, cold and still. But there had been no more snow. Just dark, flat, steel-like skies.

Underfoot, as I found when I walked up to the village shop, the snow that had fallen on Christmas Eve had compacted and turned into some sort of ice.

Before living in Sweden I had never realised that there were different kinds of ice. And different kinds of snow. In the UK it was icy or it wasn't. And usually it wasn't. Ice quickly turned to slush, as did any snow that managed to stick.

Sweden, by contrast, had a very detailed and specialised catalogue of winter conditions. And it was important that clothes were worn to match.

For instance, when the temperature hovered around -1 °C, as it often did at this time of the year, that meant wearing a surprisingly lightweight coat specially designed for everyday wear at such times. But when the temperature tumbled much further, down to -15 °C or lower, as it also did quite often, then the big quilted coats and over-trousers came out. Anything less and you would simply freeze. I loved wearing my big coat as it felt rather like going outdoors with your warm bedding still wrapped around you.

Then there were boots. Insulated, with a good grip, and easy to slip on and off. Boots like that were a mainstay in Sweden. But if there was ice – in one of its many forms – and if you wanted to walk any sort of distance, you needed to leave aside the slip-on boots and wear a pair of leather boots with soles like tractor tyres. Expensive. Padded. Rigid. These were the boots I preferred.

The odd things was, that underneath this 'advanced' clobber, you could just wear a t-shirt, jeans and ordinary socks.

A Swede once famously said "There is no such thing as bad weather, only bad clothes". And clearly they were right.

With New Year just a few days away, however, the weather did change again. And down came the thickest and fattest of snowflakes. They fell all night, all the following day, and into the second evening. Our drive disappeared from view, as did the road for a while – although every few hours a snowplough passed to re-open it.

"We're almost out of food", said Emma one day. "And with New Year coming up, the shops'll be shut. We really need to go out to the supermarket again".

She was right. One last big shop of the year would see us into early January.

The year had begun with a hopeless struggle to clear the drive of snow. But now it was just a question of making a phone call to Johan, the man with the big yellow tractor.

So I called him, and less than an hour later, the ground shook as his vast machine trundled up our drive, pushing aside everything in its path. Once again, what it didn't shove out of the way, it crunched and compacted underneath its massive wheels.

Two and a half days' snow, cleared in less than five minutes.

I went outside to pay Johan. And he clambered out of his cab to meet me. Emma came out too, to wish him all the best for the New Year.

"Hallo", said Johan, extending a huge hand towards first Emma and then me, "Did you have a good Christmas?"

We told him that we had. And that we were looking forward to a few more days off over the New Year.

Johan half turned to go but there was clearly something he wanted to say. So he turned back to us. "I saw you both on Christmas Eve. At the church in Hovmantorp."

"Oh, yes", said Emma, "We wanted to see a midnight mass. All those candles. It was so beautiful. Were you there?"

Johan nodded. "Yes. Well, I'm not so religious but because Charlotte was going to be there and sing, I was there this time. At the back. But you two, you met her?"

I glanced at Emma.

Obviously Johan was referring to the girl with the beautiful voice. But we didn't know who she was.

"Yes, er..." Emma began. "She's such a nice person".

"And a great voice", I added.

Johan nodded again. "Yes. We were all so proud of her when she won Eurovision. She has always sung".

A few minutes later, Johan and his machine were on their way back up the drive and Emma and I were running up the steps and grabbing for the internet to find out who Charlotte was and when she had won Eurovision. Was Johan right? Or had he been at the Yuletide booze? We weren't sure.

But no. He was right. Of course.

The woman who had sung so beautifully in the church, and with whom we had talked briefly, was none other than Charlotte Perelli. She had won – won! – Eurovision in 1999 and had done well in it again in 2008. She had been born Charlotte Nilsson, and had grown up – of course – in Hovmantorp. Where, presumably, she regularly returned to visit family and friends.

We both felt a bit stupid about that. We had been talking to one of the most popular singers in Sweden, and hadn't even realised it. But after dinner that evening, and a drop more wine, it just seemed sort of funny.

"Well", I said. "That's what comes from moving to a new country. We can't be expected to know everything!"

Feeling oddly happy about that encounter, and with a warm glow courtesy of that wine, I decided to take a short walk after dinner. Emma came with me.

It was dark. It was bitterly cold. And it was already quite late. So we decided we wouldn't go far. Just up towards the village a little. And then back home.

Under a blanket of snow the forest was silent. And we wondered – once more – how the wild animals survived out there during the long Swedish winter.

How did they find food under the thick snow? And what food? What was there left out there, at this time of year, for them to eat? And how did they keep warm? Especially when the wind drove in from Russia, and a freezing -10 °C dropped to a lethal -25 °C. And the snow drifted, was blown sideways and must cling to their fur coats?

It was a beautiful country. A wilderness maybe just about kept in check by the Swedes. But it was also a harsh land. The only real frontier country in western Europe.

"And Finland", added Emma.

I nodded. "Yeah. And Finland".

"And Norway must be similar. It must be hard. Even if it is mountains and not forest".

I agreed.

By now we were heading back home and had just reached the end of our drive. Going out, we had cut across our land to reach the bridle path which led to the village. But the snow on the path had been so deep, the going so hard, that we had decided to walk back along the road. The ploughs had kept it clear. But there was no traffic on it.

Our drive had been cleared too, just a few hours earlier, by Johan. But this was the first time we had walked along it since then.

"Oh", I said, stopping dead in my tracks and looking at the ground in front of me.

"Oh", said Emma, seeing it at the very same moment.

I bent down and picked up a large piece of splintered wood. Emma bent down and found another. There were several of them.

Johan's tractor was huge. And heavy. It took no prisoners in terms of snow. Whatever got in the way was sure to get shoved to one side with a lot of force.

"The gate", said Emma at last.

"The gate", I repeated, slowly.

We dug around in the snow and recovered one or two more pieces. Traditionally Sweden was a country that made matches. And Johan had just made matchsticks out of our gate.

Each holding one piece, but without saying anything else, we both continued to walk along the drive, back to the warmth of our house.

I laughed. Looked up at sky. Snow was beginning to fall, the year ending just as it had begun.

"I know!" I said. "I'll find a blacksmith. And he can make me a metal gate. After all, in a country like this, there are all kinds of traditional crafts. A nice iron gate..."

"On the other hand, it's also a very cold country", said Emma as we reached the bottom of the steps which led up to our door. She passed me the shattered piece of wood that had, briefly, been my gate. "And we can never have too much firewood".

FIN

Would you like to read MORE about SWEDEN?

If so, then why not take a look at the new FRODE books?

Set in the Swedish Iron Age, these stories are traditional, detective stories. Great reads for ALL the FAMILY.

Frode: Murder at Brae

FRODE is a trader in amber, and he is travelling to the coast to take advantage of recent storms which often wash that precious material ashore.

BUT there has been a DEATH in the nearby village of Brae, and once he is summoned by the mysterious 'Whistlers', Frode has no choice but to go along and investigate...

Frode: Retribution

FRODE meets an old friend, who tells him about a MURDER in the nearby town of Ostmar.

The killer, however, has disappeared and cannot be brought to trial.

Frode visits the town, where he finds that not everything is as it first appears...

Printed in Great Britain
by Amazon

20254427R00181